Activities
MANAGEMENT

Team Leader Development Series

Cathy Lake

OXFORD   AUCKLAND   BOSTON   JOHANNESBURG   MELBOURNE   NEW DELHI

Butterworth-Heinemann
Linacre House, Jordan Hill, Oxford OX2 8DP
225 Wildwood Avenue, Woburn, MA 01801–2041
A division of Reed Educational and Professional Publishing Ltd

A member of the Reed Elsevier plc group

First published 1999

British Library Cataloguing in Publication Data
A catalogue record for this book is available from the British Library

ISBN 0 7506 4042 1   24687049

Composition by Genesis Typesetting, Rochester, Kent
Printed and bound in Great Britain

Contents

Introduction   xi

1 Quality   1

Learning objectives   1
NVQ links   1
Introduction   2
Customers and suppliers   3
The economics of quality   6
Total Quality Management   9
Quality tools   11
Quality standards   15
Developing and implementing a quality management
system   20
Summary   23
Review and discussion questions   24
Case study   24
Work-based assignment   25
Action plan   25

2 Planning techniques   26

Learning objectives   26
NVQ links   26
Introduction   26
The planning process   27
How organizations plan   32
Setting objectives   40
The reality of planning   41
Communicating with your team   44
Scheduling techniques   48
Summary   55

Review and discussion questions 56
Case study 56
Work-based assignment 57
Action plan 57

3 Monitoring activities 58

Learning objectives 58
NVQ links 58
Introduction 58
The monitoring function 60
How do you monitor activities? 65
Problem solving 72
Updating your plans 76
Recommending improvements 81
Summary 89
Review and discussion questions 90
Case study 90
Work-based assignment 91
Action plan 91

4 Raw materials, supplies and equipment 92

Learning objectives 92
NVQ links 92
Introduction 92
Purchasing and supply systems 93
Stock control 101
Procedures for receiving goods 103
Security and care of supplies and equipment 105
Summary 108
Review and discussion questions 109
Case study 109
Work-based assignment 110
Action plan 110

5 Health and safety 111

Learning objectives 111
NVQ links 111
Introduction 111
Health and safety and the law 113
Responsibility for health and safety 116

Health and safety policy   122
Safety audit and risk assessment   123
Dealing with emergencies   126
Investigating and reporting accidents   132
Summary   135
Review and discussion questions   135
Case study   136
Work-based assignment   136
Action plan   137

6 The environment   138

Learning objectives   138
NVQ links   138
Introduction   138
Environmental legislation   139
Sources of pollution   142
Conserving natural resources   144
Conserving energy   145
Summary   148
Review and discussion questions   148
Case study   149
Work-based assignment   149
Action plan   149

Feedback   **150**

Further reading   **154**

Index   **155**

Introduction

Introduction

There are four books in the Team Leader Development Series, *People and Self Management*, *Information Management*, *Resources Management* and *Activities Management*, covering key topics from the four principal roles of management. The series has been designed to provide you with the knowledge and skills needed to carry out the role of team leader. The actual name of the job role of a team leader will vary from organization to organization. In your organization, the job role might be called any of the following:

- team leader
- supervisor
- first line manager
- section leader
- junior manager
- chargehand
- foreman
- assistant manager
- administrator.

If you work in the services or a hospital, team leaders may be called by another name not on the above list. However, in this series 'team leader' has been used throughout to describe the job role.

Who the series is intended for

If you have line-management responsibility for people within your organization, or you are hoping to progress to a position in which you will have this responsibility, then this series is for you. You may have been recently promoted into a team leader position or you may have been a team leader for some time. The series is relevant for you whether you work in a small organization or a large organization, whether you work in the public sector, private sector or voluntary sector. The books are designed to provide you with practical help which will enable you to perform better at work and to provide support to a range of programmes of study which have been designed specifically for team leaders.

Related programmes of study

There are a number of management qualifications that have been designed for team leaders. The titles in this series have been structured around the four key roles of management: Managing People, Managing Activities, Managing Resources and Managing Information. The content of each title has been developed in accordance with all the main qualifications in this area. Your tutor, manager or trainer will help you design a programme of study for your particular qualification route. Further details about each syllabus can be found in the tutor supplement that accompanies this textbook.

Activities Management covers the core topics in this key role of management detailed in the programmes of study from the National Examining Board of Supervision and Management, the Institute of Supervisory Management, Edexel and the Institute of Management who all award qualifications in Supervisory Management. The Team Leader Development Series has also been devised to provide material that is relevant for those who are working towards a NVQ or SVQ at level 3 in management. The national management standards at this level cover the full range of general management activities which all managers working in a team leader position are expected to carry out. The Team Leader Development Series covers all the core topics involved with the activities defined in each of the key roles of management listed above. Your tutor will have full details about the national standards.

The content of *Activities Management* covers the essential underpinning knowledge for the following units:

A1   Maintain activities to meet requirements
E5   Identify improvements to energy efficiency
E8   Provide advice and support for improving energy efficiency
F5   Provide advice and support for the development and implementation of quality systems
F7   Carry out quality audits

These units of competence consist of the following elements:

A1.1   Maintain work activities to meet requirements
A1.2   Maintain healthy, safe and productive working conditions
A1.3   Make recommendations for improvements to work activities
E5.1   Identify opportunities to improve energy efficiency
E5.2   Recommend improvements to energy efficiency
E8.1   Encourage involvement in energy efficiency activities
E8.2   Provide advice on the competencies needed to use energy efficiently
E8.3   Provide advice on the training needed to use energy efficiently
F7.1   Audit compliance with quality systems
F7.2   Follow-up quality audits

The work-based assignments, which can be used to gather evidence for your portfolio, are mapped to the relevant elements of competence so that you can see which elements you are working towards.

As part of your work towards a vocational qualification in management at level 3, you also have to demonstrate that you have developed a number of personal competencies (in other words, skills and attitudes) that will enable you to apply your knowledge and understanding to a range of different situations at work. You will cover the range of personal competencies in many aspects of your work. This book will be particularly helpful in providing support for the following personal competencies:

- acting assertively
- behaving ethically
- building teams
- focusing on results
- influencing others
- managing self
- thinking and taking decisions

Synopsis of *Activities Management*

The book begins with a chapter on quality – an issue that is central to the management of activities. The main principles, tools and techniques of quality management are described and there is also an introduction to ISO9000, the international standard for quality management systems. The second chapter is devoted to planning. The planning process is described, together with planning techniques that are commonly used within organizations. Monitoring is covered in the third chapter, with advice on how you can measure and control time, money and quality. There is also information on dealing with problems. The fourth chapter is concerned with managing raw materials, supplies and equipment. The issues discussed here include ordering, storage and security. The fifth chapter examines health and safety, including your legal rights and responsibilities. The final chapter considers the contribution you can make to the conservation of natural resources and to the general awareness of your colleagues, and perhaps your customers, in relation to environmental issues.

Learning structure

Each chapter begins with **Learning objectives**, a list of statements which say what you will be able to do, after you have worked through the chapter. This is followed by the 'Introduction', a few lines which introduce the material that is covered in the chapter.

There are several **Activities** in each chapter. You will find the answers at the end of the book.

There are also **Investigates** in each chapter, these are related to something which has been covered in the text. The suggestion is that you investigate the matter that has just been covered in your own organization. It is important, that you understand what you have learned, but also that you can relate what you have learned to your own organization.

Each chapter has a **Summary**, the summary recaps the main points that have been covered in the chapter, it round of the knowledge and skill areas that have been covered in the main body of the chapter, before the text moves into a range of tasks that you can complete to consolidate your learning.

There are a set of **Review and discussion questions** following the summary. You answer these after you have worked through the chapter to check whether you have understood and remembered the information that you have just read. Answers and guidelines to these questions can be found in the tutor resource material.

You are provided with an opportunity to deal with the issues raised in the chapter that you have just read by analysing the **Case study**. The case study is a scenario based in the workplace and a chance to 'practice' how you might deal with a situation at work.

There is a **Work-based assignment** at the end of each chapter, these have been designed, so that if you complete the assignment, you will be able to apply the knowledge and skills that you have covered in the chapter in the workplace. The relevant units of competence are shown in the portfolio icon where applicable. These will be of use to you if you are studying towards an S/NVQ at Level 3 in management.

Each chapter contains an **Action plan**. This is a step-by-step framework that you can use to start putting into practice some of the ideas you have been considering in the preceding chapter.

1 Quality

Learning objectives

On completion of this chapter you will be able to:

- describe the principles of quality management
- describe the principles of Total Quality Management (TQM)
- use a selection of quality management tools
- outline the requirements of ISO9001
- advise on the development and implementation of quality systems within your own department.

NVQ links

This chapter covers much of the underpinning knowledge required for the vocational qualification in management at level 3 for the optional units:

Unit F5 Provide advice and support for the development and implementation of quality systems

which consists of four elements

F5.1   Provide advice and support for the assessment of processes and working environments

F5.2   Provide advice and support for the assessment of plans to improve quality systems

F5.3   Provide advice and support for the development of measurement systems

F5.4   Provide advice and support for the collection, analysis and documentation of information.

Unit F7 Carry out quality audits

which consists of two elements

F7.1   Audit compliance with quality systems

F7.2   Follow-up quality audits.

Introduction

In everyday language, the word 'quality' is used to describe top-of-the-range, luxury items. Quality is often associated with high specifications and expense. For example, we would expect to pay more for the extra features and the high standard of workmanship we would get in a 'quality car'. However, in management terminology, 'quality' has a different meaning. It is defined as:

> *The totality of features and characteristics of a product or service that bear on its ability to satisfy stated or implied needs.*
>
> *(ISO 8402: Quality Vocabulary)*

You may also hear quality defined more concisely, as:

> *conformance to requirements.*

An even simpler definition of quality is:

> *fitness for use.*

A quality product or service is one that does the job for which it was intended. In some cases this will mean that it is produced to a high specification. However, in other situations, a high specification is not what is required. For example, if you are buying a car to drive to work every day and only have a limited budget, features such as petrol consumption, reliability and safety may be more important to you than electric windows or the ability to get from 0 to 60 in eight seconds. Quality is actually defined by the requirements of the customer.

Quality management is concerned with methods and systems to ensure that an organization meets the needs of its customers. These customers include the people who buy the organization's products and services. Quality managers also think of the organization itself as a chain of customers and suppliers, all of whom have requirements that must be met.

In this chapter you will read about the approach known as Total Quality Management. You will also find out about ISO9000, an internationally recognized standard for quality systems. You will investigate what a concern for quality means for the people who work for an organization, and consider the contribution that you can make to maintaining and improving quality within your own area of responsibility.

ACTIVITIES MANAGEMENT

Customers and suppliers

All organizations have external customers and suppliers. The customers are the people who receive the services or buy the products that the organization is in business to provide. A customer may be an individual, a group of people or another organization. Frequently, a product passes through the hands of several different customers before it reaches the end-user. For example:

- a market garden grows tomatoes and sells them to a **wholesaler**
- the wholesaler sells boxes of tomatoes to a **supermarket group**
- the supermarket group passes boxes of tomatoes on to one of its **supermarkets**
- a **customer** goes into the supermarket and buys half a kilo of tomatoes
- the customer puts a tomato into the lunch box that her **child** takes to school.

There are five customers here: the wholesaler, the supermarket group, the individual supermarket, the customer and the child. Some of these customers have purchased the tomato, while others have received it without payment. It is not necessary to pay for something in order to be a customer.

External suppliers are the people who provide the things that the organization needs in order to make its products or deliver its services. These supplies can include raw materials, components, equipment, premises, energy or even information. An agency that provides staff to work in the organization is another external supplier.

Some supplies are bought and sold many times, or passed on in other ways, before they reach the organization that uses them. There are often chains of suppliers, just like the chains of customers described above.

Activity 1

Look back at the example of the tomato. Who are the suppliers here?

See Feedback section for answer to this activity.

Every time an item changes hands, a transaction takes place, involving both a supplier and a customer. And if the customer then passes the item on to someone else, the customer

QUALITY

becomes the supplier. Unless you are the end-user of a product or service, like the child who eats the tomato with his lunch, you are almost certainly both a supplier and a customer.

All organizations know that it is important to please their external customers. If the diners at a restaurant do not like the food that is served, they will not eat there again. If a television company receives a flood of complaints from viewers, it may find it difficult to renew its franchise. It is also extremely important for an organization to have suppliers on which it can depend. For example, if the agency that supplies an office with temporary staff sends people who are incompetent or dishonest, it will be very difficult for the office to function properly.

Internal customers and suppliers

An organization is connected to other organizations by customer/supplier chains. These relationships also exist within the organization itself. Each time you receive a pack of paper for the photocopier from the stores, or ask someone from the IT department to come up and fix your computer, you are an internal customer. Each time you do something for another department within your organization, you are an internal supplier.

You may also be part of a customer/supplier chain within your own department or section. When you ask a member of your team to complete a task, you are a customer and the team member is the supplier. When your line manager asks you to prepare a report, you are the supplier and your manager is the customer. Remember, it is not necessary for money to change hands for a customer/supplier transaction to take place. All that is necessary is that some product, or some service, is provided.

Anyone who has worked in an organization knows the frustration of not being able to complete a task because another department has been incompetent or slow. If you were to receive poor service like this from an outside supplier, you would be very unlikely to use them again. However, when the service has been delivered by another part of your own organization, you do not usually have this option. One of the important ideas behind quality management is that people need to take these internal customer/supplier relationships just as seriously as those with their external customers and suppliers.

Investigate 1

Who are your internal customers?
Who are your internal suppliers?

Make two lists.

The requirements of customers

The quality expert Joseph Juran, who was one of the major figures in the development of Total Quality Management after the Second World War, identified five dimensions to quality:

- quality of design
- conformance to manufacturing standards
- lack of breakdowns
- satisfactory performance
- ease of maintenance after purchase.

It is quite easy to see how these dimensions apply to manufactured items such as fridges or computers. They are all areas where customers could have definite requirements. When you are thinking about the needs of customers in relation to other types of products, or services, a slightly different set of issues may be more appropriate. For example, here are some points you might want to consider when assessing the way a hotel receptionist deals with guests:

- consistency
- politeness
- responsiveness
- competence
- honesty.

If you were drawing up a list of your requirements for the information you receive from other departments in your organization, it might cover these points:

- adequacy
- accuracy
- how up-to-date it is
- relevancy
- organization
- comprehensibility
- presentation.

QUALITY

Investigate 2

Choose two internal suppliers and two internal customers from the lists you made earlier.

Next to each supplier, identify a product or a service that they provide. Summarize your requirements. How well do these suppliers fulfil your requirements?

Next to each customer, identify a product or a service that you provide. Summarize their requirements. How well do you think you fulfil these requirements?

You probably found it relatively easy to identify what you require from your internal suppliers. You may, however, have found it slightly more difficult to list the requirements of your internal customers. If this was the case, it probably means that you do not have sufficient information about what your internal customers want.

Another way to think about customer requirements is to divide them into two categories. **Defined requirements** are the essential specifications that are laid down in contracts and service agreements. These are the minimum requirements that are necessary. **Implied requirements** are the extras that are not usually written down, but can make a big difference to the perception of the customer. They could include:

- letters are laid out attractively
- service engineer wears clean overalls
- instruction leaflets are easy to understand
- receptionist remembers visitors' names
- letters are acknowledged promptly.

Small points like these can give the impression that an organization is genuinely interested in pleasing its external customers.

The economics of quality

An organization that gets a reputation for poor quality goods or services will lose customers. If it is a commercial business, whose aim is to make a profit, this can have very serious financial consequences. Non-commercial organizations can also suffer if they provide sub-standard products or services. They may receive expensive claims for damages from dissatisfied customers or find it difficult to obtain Government funds or commercial sponsorship. In extreme cases, poor quality can mean that an organization is forced out of business.

Because organizations know the importance of a good reputation, they usually try to make sure that the products or services that reach the customer are satisfactory. However, they may still be losing money because of quality problems. Many organizations waste a significant proportion of their revenue putting right their mistakes. Faulty products have to be discarded. Tasks have to be repeated because staff were not properly trained or briefed. Work takes longer than expected because unsuitable materials were purchased. These costs can arise because the organization is only concerned with the quality of the end-product and does not give sufficient attention to how it was achieved.

Processes

Quality management looks at what an organization does as a series of processes. Each process requires inputs and produces outputs.

Figure 1.1   Inputs ⟶ Process ⟶ Outputs

This very simple diagram can be used to describe everything that happens within an organization. Inputs are all the things that are necessary for the process to take place. They may include equipment, raw materials, staff, premises and technical knowledge. In a car assembly plant, the inputs could include components, skilled workers, the equipment on the assembly line and the factory building itself.

The outputs are the goods or services that are passed to the customer, or to other parts of the organization so that further processes can take place. In a car assembly plant, they would be the completed vehicles. In a hotel, the output would be the service provided to guests.

It is also possible to analyse the work done by a single department, or an individual, as a series of processes. If someone types a document or draws up a rota, they are performing a process that requires inputs and produces an output.

QUALITY

Investigate 3

Name two processes for which you are responsible. What are the inputs and the outputs?

One way to check quality is simply to look at the outputs. If the end-product is up to standard, it is passed on to the customer. However, this method has a serious disadvantage: the inspection is taking place at the wrong time, after the mistake has been made. Logically, if a process has been performed correctly, using the correct inputs, the output stands a very good chance of being correct, too. Quality management puts the emphasis on checking the inputs and the process itself, rather than simply inspecting the outputs. In the long run, prevention of mistakes is more effective – and usually much cheaper – than detection.

In essence, quality management is very simple.

1 Decide what the customer requires.
2 Design a process that will produce these quality outputs consistently.
3 Specify the inputs that are necessary for the process.
4 Start the operation.
5 Keep checking that the inputs, process and outputs conform to the standards you have set.

The benefits and costs of quality management

We have already mentioned many of the benefits that a concern for quality can bring. If external customers find that an organization's products or services consistently meet their requirements, demand will grow. As a result, the organization's income is likely to rise. Internal costs will fall, as less time and materials are wasted on work that has to be done again. Many organizations also find that the morale of the workforce rises. People can take a new pride in their work, especially if the organization encourages everyone to think creatively about ways of improving quality. Increased morale can lead to greater commitment, lower staff turnover and an ability to attract good employees to the organization.

There are also costs associated with quality. Management has to devote time and money to the design and setting up of a quality system. The system has to be fully documented and also reviewed periodically. Once the quality system is in place, a considerable amount of staff time will be needed to operate it. An organization may have to provide extra training for employees so that they have the appropriate skills for their tasks. Staff will also need to be trained to use quality management techniques and systems. Although organizations have to make a significant investment to ensure quality, they generally find that these costs are outweighed by the resulting benefits.

Total Quality Management

TQM is an approach that was first developed after the Second World War by the American quality experts Juran, Deming and Crosby. There was not much interest in these ideas in the West – until they were adopted by Japanese industry and proved to be spectacularly successful. It was not until the 1980s that TQM gained popularity in the USA and Europe.

TQM is based on the idea that the whole organization, from senior management to the most junior employees, must be concerned with quality. Everyone who works for the organization must continually be looking for ways to improve the quality of what they do. Emphasis is placed on measuring performance and setting new targets. TQM makes use of a group of problem-solving and statistical techniques, which are described later in this chapter. Teams of workers are encouraged to analyse the root cause of problems and come up with creative solutions. Good communication and recognition of success are also important features of TQM.

The work of a small group of experts, often referred to as the 'quality gurus' has been very influential in the development of TQM.

Dr W. Edwards Deming

Deming believed that managers should be the driving force for quality within an organization. He thought that management must create a culture in which inter-departmental barriers are broken down, fear is driven out and everyone is encouraged to take a pride in their work. He proposed that managers should work to set up a 'new climate', consisting of three elements:

- joy in work
- innovation
- co-operation.

QUALITY

Organizations should stop depending on inspection to discover errors after they had happened. Everyone should be involved in education and self-improvement and should work to transform the organization.

Joseph Moses Juran

Juran developed a three-stage approach called the 'Quality Planning Road Map' which describes the steps that an organization should take to promote quality.

Quality planning
- start by identifying the organization's customers
- determine their needs
- translate these needs into the organization's language
- develop a product that responds to these needs
- optimize the features of the product so that it meets the needs of customers and the organization.

Quality improvement
- develop a process that is able to produce the product
- optimize the process.

Quality control
- prove that the process can produce the product under operating conditions
- transfer the process to operations.

Philip B. Crosby

Crosby believed that companies spent a very significant amount of money making mistakes, which resulted in tasks having to be done again. He estimated that manufacturers wasted about 20 per cent of their revenue in this way. According to Crosby, service companies spent about 35 per cent of their operating expenses on doing things again that had been done incorrectly.

Crosby is associated with the concepts 'Do it Right First Time' and 'Zero Defects'. He believed that prevention of quality problems should replace detection. Managers should take the lead in encouraging the workforce to make continuous improvements.

How sympathetic do you think the senior management of your organization is to the ideas of the 'quality gurus'? How do you think your own team would react? What do **you** think of these ideas?

Some people find that the jargon associated with TQM is initially off-putting. However, it can be an exciting and fulfilling experience to work for an organization that is genuinely committed to this approach. TQM cannot succeed unless senior management makes this commitment. They will have to devote large amounts of time and money to training and the development of new attitudes among the workforce.

Quality tools

We will now examine some of the tools and techniques that are used in quality management. Brainstorming, Pareto analysis and Fishbone diagrams are all problem-solving tools. Statistical Process Control is a method for monitoring processes.

Brainstorming

This is a technique for generating ideas from a group of people. It can produce a large number of ideas in a short amount of time and is often used to find solutions to problems or to think of new ways of doing things. In a brainstorming session, one individual can sometimes build on an idea that someone else has suggested and come up with a much more creative solution than he or she could when working alone. Brainstorming is a good way of allowing staff with first-hand knowledge of a process to share their expertise.

The ideal number for a brainstorming session is between four and eight people. If the group is too large, some members may be intimidated. If the group is too small, one or two members may dominate. Everyone present should have some knowledge that they can contribute. Everyone should be familiar with the rules before the session begins.

The rules of brainstorming
• Set a time limit – about ten minutes is usually enough.
• The leader writes the topic to be brainstormed on a flip chart, where everyone can see it.

- People take turns to offer ideas.
- All ideas are recorded as they are suggested.
- People must not criticize or discuss other's ideas.
- All ideas – however outlandish – are welcome.
- People can build on other people's ideas.

At the end of ten minutes you will probably have a large collection of ideas, a few of which are worth further investigation.

Pareto analysis

This method of analysis is based on the phenomenon that, in a surprisingly large number of situations, 80 per cent of the effects arise from 20 per cent of the causes. For example, about 80 per cent of the breakdowns are likely to happen to about 20 per cent of the delivery vans. About 80 per cent of the calls to a customer service line are likely to come from around 20 per cent of customers. The method was developed by Vilfredo Pareto, a nineteenth-century economist, who noticed that 80 per cent of the wealth in Italy was owned by 20 per cent of the population.

A Pareto analysis is a method of examining data to identify the 20 per cent of causes that are responsible for 80 per cent of the problems. Once these key causes have been found, corrective action can be directed at them.

Activity 3

Figure 1.2 was drawn up from data collected from a customer survey. It shows the percentage of people that gave various reasons for not renewing a service contract with a central heating company.

Figure 1.2

A   service representative was not on time for appointment
B   system did not need servicing
C   rival company offered cheaper deal
D   system no longer in use
E   customer did not receive reminder
F   service representative left house untidy
G   customer serviced system themselves
H   servicing had been inadequate
I   did not like service representative

Study Figure 1.2. What aspect or aspects of the servicing arrangements should the management of the company try to improve?

See Feedback section for answer to this activity.

Organizations have only limited resources at their disposal. Pareto analysis is a method of concentrating these resources in areas where they will be most effective.

Fishbone diagrams

Fishbone diagrams, also known as Ishikawa diagrams after their inventor, are used to think about possible causes of problems. The problem or effect that you are investigating is written in a box on the right, with an arrow pointing to it. The next step is to think of various categories into which the possible causes could fall. These could be:

- people
- processes
- materials
- equipment.

Arrows representing these categories are added to the diagram. Finally, the causes themselves are added. A finished diagram might look like Figure 1.3 on page 14.

Statistical Process Control

Statistical Process Control, or SPC, is a system of taking samples to monitor whether a process is working correctly or

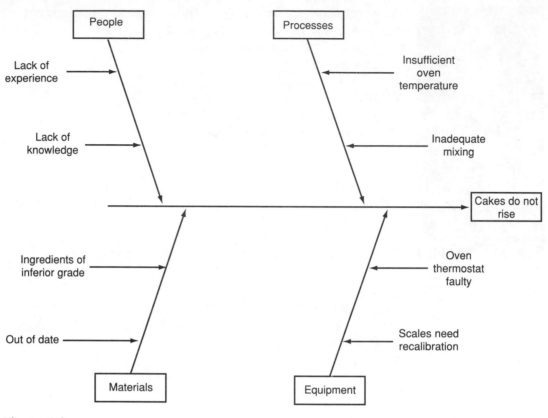

Figure 1.3

needs adjusting. As its name suggests, SPC demands specialized statistical knowledge. However, the basic principles are quite straightforward.

If you make a large number of measurements, such as the diameter of a component produced by a machine, you will find that they fall into a pattern. Most of the results will be clustered around a central figure, known as the **mean**. A few results would be significantly larger than the mean, and a few would be smaller. If you then take sample measurements, perhaps measuring one in a hundred of the components that the machine produces, these measurements will fall into the same pattern as the original measurements. If the pattern of the samples is different, this suggests that something has gone wrong with the process. It could be that the machine needs adjusting, or that it is being operated incorrectly.

It is obviously impracticable to have a trained statistician on a factory floor, monitoring the components as they come off a machine. However, control charts can be prepared from statistical data which can be used by ordinary workers to check that the process is working properly. Figure 1.4 is an example:

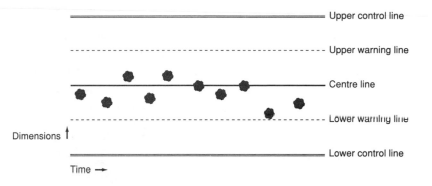

Figure 1.4

Sample measurements are taken over a period of time and added to the chart. If measurements cross either of the warning lines, the operative knows that the process may be moving off course and should be watched carefully. If either of the control lines is crossed, it may be time to take action. SPC is used most frequently in manufacturing, but it can be used in any situation in which a similar operation is performed over and over again.

Quality standards

There are some situations in which an organization needs to be absolutely sure that it is meeting specified quality levels. These situations include the way that staff are appointed and dismissed, health and safety matters and the issue of equal opportunities. You will study these areas elsewhere in your course. There are also some standards that only apply to specific industries. For example, a restaurant must be able to show that food is stored at correct temperatures and that other health and safety regulations are being followed. A hospital must be able to show that it is following accepted procedures in the treatment of patients. An organization that arranges foster care must run appropriate checks on the people to whom it assigns children. A company that sells pensions must ensure that its representatives are properly trained and follow agreed procedures. Some of these procedures are laid down in legislation. Others may be produced by professional and trade associations and appear in the form of charters or guidelines.

QUALITY

| Investigate 4 | Make a list of the legislation and guidelines that apply specifically to the type of work done by the organization that you work for. |

An organization that fails to meet these obligatory standards can face prosecution or even closure. It is essential to have systems in place to check that these standards are being met. It is also necessary to have adequate documentation to prove that these systems are in operation.

ISO9000

When an organization places a contract with another business, it frequently asks for details of the quality control system that is in place. Some organizations develop their own methods of monitoring and improving quality. Others choose to adopt a system that has official, international recognition.

ISO9000 has its roots in some standards that were produced in the 1950s by the Ministry of Defence. The MoD wanted to reduce the frequency with which equipment failed when it was being used in the field. It did this by laying down standards to be used by the contractors who manufactured the equipment. These standards were developed and adopted in other NATO countries and then extended to companies who had no connection with the defence industry. These NATO standards formed the basis of British Standard, BS5750, which was developed in 1979 and is still in use. BS5750 was adopted internationally and is now known as ISO9000.

ISO9000 is made up of three major parts:

- ISO9001 – specification for design, development, production, installation and servicing. This is the most comprehensive standard. It includes the specifications contained in ISO9002. Organizations that provide services, as well as those that manufacture products, can use it.
- ISO9002 – specification for production and installation. Organizations that manufacture and deliver products, but are not involved in the original design, can restrict themselves to this part of the standard.
- ISO9003 – specification for final inspection and test. This part is only relevant for organizations whose product has already been manufactured elsewhere and only needs to be inspected and tested before it is supplied.

Contents of ISO9001

Here is a summary of the requirements of ISO9001.

1 Quality policy	Senior management must design and publish a quality policy. This should give the organization's quality objectives.
2 Organization	All the roles and responsibilities that affect quality must be defined. A manager must be made responsible for the quality management system. Quality audit procedures must be set up.
3 Quality system	A quality management system must be designed and set up.
4 Contract review	The organization must check that it is able to fulfil the requirements of a contract before it accepts it. These requirements must be clearly stated in writing.
5 Design control	The design process, including planning procedures, inputs, outputs, verification and design changes, must be fully documented.
6 Document control	Procedures must be set up for issuing and amending documents. Documents should only be drawn up or altered by the people who are authorized to do so and should only be circulated to the people who are authorized to see them. There must be a system for withdrawing out-of-date versions of documents.
7 Purchasing	Supplies should only be purchased from approved suppliers. Checks should be made to ensure that suppliers are capable of meeting requirements.
8 Products supplied by customers	If customers supply goods to be worked on, there must be a procedure to check, identify, securely store these goods and use them as specified in the contract.

QUALITY

9 Product identification and traceability	There must be procedures to identify components and products throughout the manufacturing process.
10 Process control	Before production begins, full instructions must be prepared. These should cover start-up procedures, the order in which activities should be carried out, materials and equipment required, the method of monitoring the process, maintenance and how the product will be assessed or tested at the end of the process.
11 Inspection and testing	Inspection and testing should be carried out when goods and materials are received, while the process is going on and after the process has finished. All inspections and tests should be fully documented.
12 Inspection, measuring and test equipment	Any equipment used in the inspection process must be regularly checked and calibrated. Full records must be kept.
13 Inspection and test status	Products and components must be labelled so that everyone involved knows whether they are waiting to be tested, have passed inspection or have failed inspection.
14 Control of non-conforming product	Products or services that fail inspections must be clearly labelled to ensure they are not used. There must be a procedure for dealing with products that fail inspection. This may involve scrapping, reworking, repairing or using the product in another way.
15 Corrective action	There must be systems to avoid the recurrence of problems. This will include investigating the causes of errors and introducing corrective action.
16 Handling, storage, packaging and delivery	There must be procedures to ensure that products are adequately packed, handled and stored.

17 Quality records	Procedures should exist describing what quality records are kept, how they are stored and retrieved and the amount of time for which they are retained.
18 Internal quality audits	There must be procedures for managers to review the quality management system and make sure that it still meets requirements. There must also be quality audits to check that everyone is following the system.
19 Training	There should be a system to identify what training is necessary for any activity affecting the quality of a product or service. Individuals should have access to the appropriate procedures, tools and skills to carry out tasks in accordance with requirements.
20 Servicing	If the customer requires after-sales support, procedures should be in place to ensure that work meets requirements.
21 Statistical techniques	If statistical techniques are used to check products or processes, they should be fully documented, understood by the people concerned and, wherever possible, based on recognized techniques.

Investigate 5

Which of the procedures described in ISO9001 do you already follow in your own work? Make a list.

Even if your organization is not following the detailed specifications laid down in ISO9001, it probably uses many of the procedures mentioned here.

QUALITY

Developing and implementing a quality management system

Three levels of document are necessary for a quality management system that meets the requirements of ISO9001:

- a quality manual
- process procedures
- work instructions.

The **quality manual** is a statement produced by senior management that describes the organization's quality policy and its objectives for each of the requirements of ISO9001. The quality manual is usually not longer than about 20 pages. It does not go into a great deal of detail and is often used to give customers and staff an overall appreciation of the organization's approach to quality.

The **procedures** go into much more detail than the quality manual. They describe each process, usually giving the following information:

- what the process is intended to do
- how it operates
- the controls that are in place to ensure that the output is of consistent quality
- how the procedure meets the requirements of ISO9001.

Work instructions are detailed instructions for the use of staff who are to carry out tasks. ISO9001 only demands work instructions in situations where their absence would endanger quality. It is not necessary to prepare instructions for every activity that takes place. The amount of detail that they give will depend on the experience of the staff who will be using them.

If you are a junior manager, it is unlikely that you will be asked to contribute directly to the quality manual. However, you may well be asked to draw up procedures and prepare work instructions. In the remainder of this chapter we will consider some of the issues you should consider if you are asked to advise on your organization's quality management system.

Assessing processes

The first thing to consider is the purpose that the process is intended to achieve. This purpose will involve producing an output that meets the requirements of internal or external customers. It may be necessary to check these requirements with your customers. Their needs may have changed since they were last consulted – or they may never have been asked about their requirements at all.

You should also consider how consistently the process achieves its purpose and whether this level of consistency is acceptable. If the process fails to do what it is supposed to do, you will need to investigate the causes of failure. The problem-solving tools used in TQM may be helpful here.

You also need to think about the people who operate the process. It is important that they understand what they are trying to achieve. It may be that you will have to give them more information. If the staff who are operating the process do not have the necessary skills or experience to perform their task, you may have to arrange staff development.

You should look at the inputs that the process requires. Are they of an adequate standard? If not, you will need to specify exactly what you need and negotiate with your suppliers to make sure that this standard is met consistently.

Investigate 6

Make an assessment of one of the processes for which you are responsible. What recommendations can you make to senior management?

Procedures

Procedures are frequently drawn up by people who have very little contact with the day-to-day realities of an operation. As a result, they are often unnecessarily complicated and are consequently ignored by the people who are supposed to follow them. In fact, 'working to rule' used to be a recognized tactic employed by trade unions to disrupt the work of an organization!

It is important that a procedure is realistic and achievable within a normal working routine. If you try to legislate for every eventuality, you will produce a document that is of little practical use.

Work instructions

The instructions provided for the people operating the systems need to be written in a way that they can understand.

Like the procedures, the instructions should not be unnecessarily complicated. They should be accurate, up-to-date and presented in a helpful way.

Lists giving numbered steps and simple flow diagrams can help people to understand the sequence in which they should do things. Lists of 'do's and don'ts' can also be helpful in some situations. It is also very important for staff to be able to identify the problems they are expected to sort out for themselves and those that they should refer to a supervisor or more experienced colleague.

Investigate 7

Write a set of work instructions for a new employee, explaining how to perform a simple process. Show the result to a colleague. Can he or she suggest any improvements?

Inspection and measurement

Decisions will have to be made about the points at which inputs, outputs and the process itself are inspected and measured. Too little inspection can allow mistakes to slip through. Too much can become a burden and hold up the production process. You will have to decide:

- what is checked
- when it is checked
- how often it is checked
- by whom it is checked.

Generally, it is best if checks are performed by someone as close to the production process as possible. Ideally, most of the checking should be done by the person who is actually operating the process.

Auditing a quality system

A large part of your day-to-day work is likely to be concerned with ensuring that the quality management system is working effectively. From time to time, you may also be asked to perform an audit of the system itself. In this situation, useful questions include:

- How aware of the quality system are people at an operational level?
- How seriously do they take it?
- Do they understand its importance?
- In a crisis, are quality standards sacrificed?
- What happens to a member of staff who does not follow the quality system?

You should also consider how seriously you take the quality system yourself. If you are tempted to ignore parts of it because they are outdated or irrelevant, you should draw these shortcomings in the system to the attention of your line manager.

Summary

The quality of a product or service is the extent to which it conforms to the requirements of the customer. An organization has external customers and suppliers. Within your own organization, you also have internal customers and suppliers. Quality management involves analysing what an organization does in terms of a series of processes. It is important to set standards for the input to the process, and the way the process is carried out, as well as for the outputs. In this way, an organization can improve the quality of its products and services and also reduce waste.

TQM is an approach to quality management that gained popularity in Japan. It involves encouraging a concern for quality throughout the organization and cannot succeed without the wholehearted commitment of senior management. TQM makes use of a group of tools and techniques to investigate problems and monitor activities. They include brainstorming, Pareto analysis, Fishbone diagrams and SPC.

Some organizations seek validation of their quality management systems under the international standard ISO9000, which is equivalent to the British Standard BS5750. The demands of ISO9000 are extremely rigorous. The documentation that an organization must produce includes a quality manual, process procedures and work instructions. It is possible that you will have an important role to play in developing your organization's procedures and work instructions.

Review and discussion questions

1 What are the advantages to an organization of taking quality management seriously?
2 What are the three stages in Juran's 'Quality Planning Road Map'?
3 In what circumstances might one use a control chart?
4 List eight issues that are covered by ISO9001.
5 What differences are there between a quality manual, a process procedure and a work instruction?

Case study

You have just taken on a job as a team leader in charge of an administrative office within a medium-sized organization. You quickly discover that your department has a very poor reputation with other staff and is known for delay and inefficiency. In fact, it is a bit of a running joke. Staff turnover is very high – administrative staff rarely stay for more than three months. You want to improve this situation.

The organization does not have a Quality Manager and there is no organization-wide approach to quality control procedures. You speak to a senior manager who says she would be very interested in improving quality standards within your department, as long as you could come up with some ideas about how to do it.

- Where would you start?
- In what areas would it be useful to introduce quality standards?
- How would you encourage your team to become involved in quality improvement?

ACTIVITIES MANAGEMENT

Work-based assignment

Investigate the quality procedures that are in place within your department.

- How are they linked to the organization's quality management system?
- What legislation or other external quality standards (such as industry guidelines) do they reflect?
- Do you think that they provide adequate control of quality?

Suggest some ways in which they could be developed to increase the quality of the services or products provided by your department.

Action plan

This action plan can be used to develop a quality product or service that will meet the requirements of internal or external customers.

1 Identify your customers.
2 Identify their requirements.
3 Decide how you can best respond to these requirements.
4 Develop a product or service.
5 Develop a process that will produce this product or service.
6 Identify the inputs you will need for the process.
7 Specify your requirements for these inputs and negotiate with your suppliers to obtain them.
8 Set up the process and test it under operational conditions.

QUALITY

2 Planning techniques

Learning objectives

On completion of this chapter you will be able to:

- describe the planning cycle
- formulate, implement, monitor and evaluate a plan
- outline the planning process used within an organization
- identify planning techniques used by senior management
- set SMART objectives
- use a variety of techniques to communicate plans to your team
- draw up a schedule using a flowchart, network diagram or Gantt chart.

NVQ links

This chapter covers underpinning knowledge required for the vocational qualification in management at level 3 for the mandatory unit:

Unit A1 Maintain activities to meet requirements

A1.1   Maintain work activities to meet requirements
A1.3   Make recommendations for improvements to work activities.

Introduction

Plans play a central role in the lives of managers. All managers spend a large proportion of their time drawing up plans for the future, communicating their contents to other people and then, when the plans are put into operation, reporting back on progress.

But why are plans so important? They have many uses. To begin with, they allow people to think seriously about what they want – and what it is possible – to achieve. They also allow managers to calculate the resources, such as staff, equipment and supplies, that they will need. They are an excellent way of ensuring that all these resources are used to maximum effect.

A plan can help any group of people, whether it is the board of directors of a large company or a team of telephone sales staff, to focus on what they are supposed to be doing. It can provide a sense of purpose and the motivation to achieve more than the individuals concerned might otherwise have thought possible. If people understand how they fit into a larger plan, their own day-to-day tasks may take on more significance and value.

As a team leader, you will be responsible for carrying out plans that have been drawn up elsewhere in your organization. Typically, your line manager will indicate the objectives that your team needs to achieve by a certain time. You will probably be given a budget and other resources, such as an allocation of staff and equipment, with which to achieve these objectives. As a team leader, you will play a small, but crucial, part in the realization of your organization's plans.

In order to achieve the objectives you have been set, you will also need to draw up plans for yourself and your team. These plans are likely to be on a smaller scale and be concerned with a shorter timeframe than the plans that are prepared by the people who manage you, but they still require the use of planning skills.

As you will see in this chapter, planning requires essentially the same skills at whatever level in an organization it is undertaken. By developing your own practical abilities as a planner, you should also gain a deeper understanding of the priorities and concerns of the managers who make plans at a senior level within your organization. You will also learn something about the way that organizations formulate their long-term plans and this should, in turn, increase your appreciation of the importance of your own part in carrying out these plans.

The planning process

In essence, a plan is an account of how you intend to get from where you are at the moment to the position where you want to be. The basic elements of the planning process are exactly the same, whether you are deciding how to reorganize the office furniture or drawing up the investment strategy of a multinational company.

The planning process begins when you become aware that you are not satisfied with your present position. There may be some positive change that you want to make:

I'd really like to visit Australia.

A workplace crèche could be a real asset to this company.

Or you may be forced to take action because you are facing a problem of some kind:

While my wrist is in plaster and I can't use the car, I am going to have to find a different way of getting into work.

Unless we find a way of increasing uptake of our services, we will not be able to maintain these staffing levels for much longer.

At first, you may only have a very general idea of what you want your plan to achieve. Most plans start in this way, with some sort of 'vision' or overall picture of the goal. It is only at a later stage in the process that the details are worked out.

Whatever you are planning, you need to go through these stages:

1 identify your goal
2 clarify your present position
3 consider the range of strategies that you could use to achieve your goal
4 select the most appropriate strategy
5 break your strategy down into smaller steps.

Imagine that you are thinking about visiting a supplier at the other end of the country. Your planning process would probably go something like this:

1 *identify your goal:* I need to arrive at 11 a.m. in a relaxed and alert frame of mind
2 *clarify your present position:* I'm 250 miles away and I've got a tremendous amount of work on at the moment. There is about £100 in the budget set aside for this trip

3 *consider the range of strategies that you could use to achieve your goal:* I could make an early start and drive up in my own car. Or I could drive up the night before and stay in a hotel. I could take the plane. And there is also a morning train that would get me there in time

4 *select the most appropriate strategy:* I don't want a long car journey before the meeting and driving at night makes me tense. If I take the plane I'll go over budget and have to clear it with my line manager, who is not going to be happy. I'll take the train and get some work done on the journey

5 *break your strategy down into smaller steps:* I'll book the train now and order a taxi to pick me up at home at 6 a.m. and take me to the station.

Activity 4

Identify a simple task that you will shortly have to perform at work for the first time. Apply the five stages of the planning process to it.

The directors and senior managers within your organization go through a very similar process in their own planning meetings:

1 *identify the goal:* they decide the overall direction in which the organization should develop

2 *clarify the present position:* they look at the strengths and weaknesses of the organization at the moment and the opportunities and threats that face it

3 *consider the range of strategies that they could use to achieve the goal:* they investigate a range of business strategies, from the consolidation of an existing market to unrelated diversification, that could be used to achieve the organization's goal

4 *select the most appropriate strategy:* they decide which of these strategies is most likely to achieve the goal

5 *break the strategy down into smaller steps:* they bring in departmental managers to produce operational plans, who in turn involve team leaders to draw up shorter-term plans.

In the next section of this chapter we will look in more detail at how organizations formulate their plans.

PLANNING TECHNIQUES

The planning cycle

The drawing up of a plan is the first stage in a four-stage cycle:

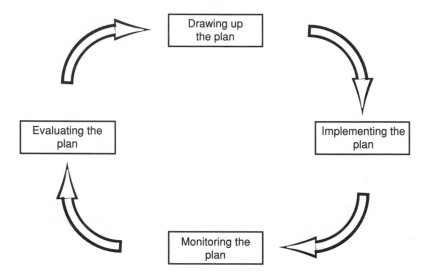

Figure 2.1

Drawing up the plan

You have already considered the five steps you should use when drawing up a plan. At the end of this chapter we will look at some tools and techniques you can use at this stage in the process.

Implementing the plan

At this point, the plan must be communicated to the people who will carry it out. Resources, such as staff, equipment and cash, are committed to the plan and put in place.

Monitoring the plan

Monitoring takes place while the planned activity is actually happening. It involves measuring progress against the objectives that were laid down at the start. Chapter 3 looks at monitoring in more detail, but it is important to consider the monitoring stage of the cycle before it is actually underway.

ACTIVITIES MANAGEMENT

In business, the most widely used monitoring tools are the **budget** and the **schedule**. As you saw in Chapter 1, it is also essential to monitor the quality of the work that is being done. The budget is a list of monetary amounts, presented under a series of headings, that you expect to spend or receive. As the activity progresses, actual amounts are added. By keeping watch on the difference (known as the **variance**) between the budgeted and actual figures, it is possible to see whether the activity is costing more (or less) than expected. The dates on which money is paid can also reveal important information about whether the activity is going forward quickly enough. We will examine budgets in more detail in Chapter 3.

The schedule is a list of dates at which particular events are supposed to happen. Schedules are often presented in the form of charts or diagrams and can be used as planning tools in their own right. We will look at how to use schedules in this way later in the chapter. In the monitoring stage of the planning cycle, a schedule provides a guide to the speed at which things are proceeding.

It is essential to identify things to monitor that will provide really useful information about how the plan is progressing. These indicators must be selected before the activity begins. If monitoring reveals that the plan is not working as anticipated, then the plan has to be amended. A good plan is flexible enough to allow some changes to be made.

Evaluating the plan

After the activity is over, it is time to consider what went well and what could have been improved. A series of questions should be asked, including:

- did we achieve our objectives?
- what mistakes did we make – and how could we avoid them next time?
- could we have used resources more effectively or more efficiently?
- were the objectives themselves worth achieving?
- were our objectives ambitious enough?

If the planned activity is a one-off project, this evaluation happens at the end, after the final product has been delivered. If the activity is continuing, it is still important to evaluate it at regular intervals. Depending on what the activity is, this may be done on a yearly, quarterly or monthly basis. The information that an evaluation reveals is used when the next plan is drawn up, and so the cycle continues.

Think about a plan that you were responsible for carrying out. What did you learn from your mistakes? Were you able to use these lessons to improve the quality of a similar plan that was drawn up subsequently?

How organizations plan

We will now examine some of the principles and techniques that organizations use when formulating their plans. By the end of this section, you should have a clear idea of your own role within the planning structure of your organization.

Levels of plan

Planning takes place at all levels of management. However, the plans made by senior, middle and junior managers have different characteristics:

- **senior managers** usually draw up long-term plans with a wide scope, involving many parts of the organization. These top-level plans frequently do not contain much detail
- **middle level managers** are concerned with medium-term plans with a more limited scope, usually only relating to their own department. These plans contain more detail
- **junior managers**, such as yourself, are responsible for short-term plans with a very limited scope but a high degree of detail.

Management experts describe these various levels of plans in a variety of different ways, but you are likely to come across the following terminology.

The mission statement

This is a broad statement of how the organization sees itself and what it is trying to achieve. Mission statements usually contain these elements:

- a description of the business the organization is in
- what the organization is trying to achieve
- a very general indication of how it intends to do this
- some mention of the values of the organization.

Mission statements vary in length. They can be a few hundred words long, or as short as a single sentence or phrase. They are usually displayed prominently on the organization's leaflets and other literature. Here are two examples of short mission statements:

> *Bringing world class service to the bakery packaging industry*

> *Contributing to the prosperity of Cornwall through providing quality education and training*

Investigate 8

What is your organization's mission statement? Does it contain the four elements described here?

Senior management often invest much time and effort in writing the mission statement and place a great deal of importance on the fact that everyone who works for the organization is familiar with what it says. Mission statements are intended to inspire people – and they are also the cornerstone on which the rest of the planning structure depends.

Strategic plans

These are the long-term, large-scale plans that are devised by senior management. They do not contain much detail, but give a general indication of what the organization intends to do to achieve its goals. There are many different types of strategy. Here, for example, are the strategies for diversification and growth that were described by the business expert Ansoff in the 1950s:

	PRODUCTS	
MARKETS	EXISTING	NEW
EXISTING	market consolidation and penetration	product development
NEW	market development	unrelated diversification

PLANNING TECHNIQUES

Market consolidation and penetration involve working with existing products in existing markets. Product development brings new products to an existing market. Market development, as the name suggests, involves developing new markets for an existing product. Unrelated diversification develops a new product for a new market.

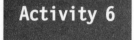

Which of Ansoff's strategies do you think would be most risky for an organization? Which would be the least risky?

See Feedback section for answer to this activity.

Once senior management has chosen its strategy, it draws up some specific strategic objectives. These will describe what the organization intends to achieve by a particular time. For example, a strategic objective could state that a company will:

> *increase the number of outlets in the South of England to twenty by the end of three years*

A strategic plan would describe, in outline terms, how this objective could be achieved.

Operational plans

Once senior management has drawn up the strategic plans, a series of operational objectives can be prepared. These objectives will detail what each department or section of the organization has to do within the strategic plan. For example, the company that wanted to increase its outlets in the South of England might set the following operational objective for the Human Resources Department (HRD):

> *double the number of staff on the management trainee scheme in twelve months time.*

An operational plan is a description of how an operational objective is to be achieved. Typically, it has a time scale of 1 year. It includes information on the resources that will be required and how they will be used. It also provides the basis for more detailed planning that takes place at a supervisory level.

Action plans

This is the type of planning that you are most likely to be involved in yourself. It takes place at a team leader level and is usually concerned with what has to happen on a week-by-week, or even day-by-day, basis. Action plans are descriptions of how team objectives are to be achieved. These team objectives are derived from the operational plan. Here, for example, is a team objective that arose from the HRD's plan to double the number of staff on the management trainee scheme:

send out a new version of the leaflet describing the management trainee scheme by the end of September

Here is an action plan setting out the steps to be taken to fulfil this objective:

Action	By whom	By when
1 Write copy	CM	20.8
2 Copy checked for accuracy	RR	22.8
3 Leaflet designed	EWL	30.8
4 Photographs taken	EWL	6.9
5 Desktop publishing of leaflet	EWL	13.9
6 Proofs checked	RR, CM	16.9
7 Leaflet printed	TT	23.9

As you can see, each action is accompanied by the initials of the person who is responsible for completing it and a date by which it must be finished. If it would be helpful to people, you could also give the start date for each of these activities. If you only give one set of dates, it is important to be very clear about whether these are the start or finish dates. At the end of this chapter we will look at techniques you can use to put together a plan of this kind.

Management by objectives

You will have noticed that all the stages in the planning process, from the overall mission statement to the day-to-day action plans, are linked to each other. Ideally, every manager knows exactly what he or she ought to be doing in order to help the organization achieve its long-term mission. In real life, day-to-day events can make people lose sight of the larger perspective.

Management by objectives is a method that was developed by Peter Drucker in the 1950s. It links the personal goals of individual managers with the goals of the organization as a whole.

Each manager, in discussion with his or her own immediate manager, draws up a list of key tasks. This list is used to prepare a short list of objectives on which the manager should concentrate his or her efforts. Each objective is presented in the form of a standard that can be measured. For example, a manager's objectives could include:

> *reduce customer complaints by 50 per cent*

> *reduce the time it takes to service internal orders to two working days*

At the end of a set period, the manager and his or her line manager meet to discuss how well he or she has performed. Any problems are examined and new objectives are agreed for the next period.

Investigate 9

Is your own performance assessed in this way? If so, how useful do you think this process is for you? If not, what objectives would you like to set for yourself?

Some management planning techniques

We will now take a look at some of the techniques that managers use during the planning process. The methods we describe here are used to gain an understanding of the current situation and to predict what is likely to happen in the future. At the end of this chapter, we will examine techniques that can be used to produce a step-by-step plan.

STEP factors

Every organization is influenced by the world outside. STEP factors are the:

- **S**ocial
- **T**echnological
- **E**conomic
- **P**olitical

forces that can have an effect on an organization.

Social factors include changes in attitudes and behaviour in society and the way that the population as a whole is made up. For example, a fashion for body piercing or a growing number of retired people with large disposable incomes would both be described as social changes. Social factors may have an effect on the market for an organization's products or services. They may also affect the way an organization treats its employees.

Technological factors include new materials and processes. They may affect the quality of goods and services that customers expect and the internal costs that the organization has to meet. For example, a hotel could find that all its competitors are now using an extremely efficient computerized booking system and decide that it was likely to lose business if it did not follow this trend.

Economic factors are, as the name suggests, related to money. They include the money that customers have available, the rates of pay expected by staff, levels of inflation, interest rates and international exchange rates. All these things can have a powerful impact on the funds that an organization has available.

Political factors are often related to Government legislation. They also include local government policies and actions and the effect of international relations. A local council's decision to refuse planning permission for a new factory and a war on the other side of the world would both be classed as political factors.

| Activity 7 | What STEP factors are most likely to affect your organization? |

PLANNING TECHNIQUES

STEP factors can be difficult to predict, but large organizations like to keep an eye on emerging trends in all these areas.

SWOT analysis

This is a method of focusing on an organization's position. SWOT stands for:

- **S**trengths
- **W**eaknesses
- **O**pportunities
- **T**hreats.

The strengths and weaknesses refer to the internal conditions of the organization. For example, a highly trained workforce would be considered a strength, while outdated equipment that keeps breaking down would be considered a weakness. The opportunities and threats are those presented by the outside environment. They are the key STEP factors you have just been considering.

In a SWOT analysis, notes are made under these four headings. The aim is to find a way forward that maximizes the opportunities that are available to the organization while correcting major weaknesses and avoiding the threats.

Activity 8

Make notes for a SWOT analysis of your organization. What recommendations would you make for the way it should develop in the future?

You are unlikely to be asked to participate in a SWOT analysis for your organization, but you may find that this technique can also give you some useful insights into the way in which your own team needs to develop in the future.

Forecasting

All organizations want to know how much money they will have available in the future. Without this information, it is very difficult to make plans. Organizations that rely for their income on selling their goods and services try to forecast future sales. The details of the methods used to produce forecasts are beyond the scope of this book, but it is useful to know something about the basic principles involved.

- **Last period forecasting**: this is the simplest way to make a forecast. It is based on the idea that if you sold fifty cars this month, you will sell fifty cars next month. However, in most businesses, sales vary from month to month.
- **Moving average forecasting**: this method is likely to produce a more accurate forecast. It involves taking an average of the last few months' figures. Usually, one looks at the figures for the previous three months.
- **Weighted moving average forecasting**: if sales are following an upward or downward trend, the most recent figures are likely to be more significant than those from three months ago. This method is also based on averaging past results, but it gives more weight to more recent figures.
- **Indexed four quarter moving average**: this method is used when figures change dramatically with the seasons. For example, a manufacturer of sun creams will make more sales in the summer and it would be useless for this company to use an ordinary moving average method of forecasting, based on sales made in the previous three months. However, the sales figures from twelve months ago may be too out of date to be useful. This method takes the average figure for the last year and then multiplies it by an index figure. This index figure represents the relationship between sales in a particular quarter and the average of sales for the whole year.

When making forecasts, senior managers must also think about limiting factors. These are the fixed factors that can limit expansion or change. They might include:

- the amount of money that an organization is able to borrow in order to finance new investments
- the size of the market
- the capacity of the plant and machinery available
- the number of skilled people in the workforce
- the availability of raw materials
- the size of the site.

Investigate 10

What limiting factors affect your organization?

Setting objectives

An objective is a statement of what is to be achieved. Objectives can be set for whole organizations, departments, teams or individual members of staff. Objectives should be SMART:

- *Simple* – so that everyone concerned can understand them
- *Measurable* – so that you will know whether or not they have been achieved
- *Achievable* – based on what you estimate that you (or the people concerned) are likely to be able to do
- *Realistic* – taking into account the internal and external factors that may influence the situation
- *Time-related* – so that you will have a time scale against which to measure progress.

Think of an objective or target that you set for your team that was **not** met. Why was it not achieved?

It is quite difficult to write an objective that meets all these requirements. In practice, many people draw up objectives that are too ambitious, or are phrased so vaguely that it is difficult to know whether or not they have been achieved.

Peter Drucker identified seven areas in which most organizations set objectives:

- profitability
- market share and standing
- productivity
- management and employee performance
- technical innovation
- social and public responsibility
- resource utilization.

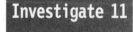

What can you find out about your organization's objectives in these seven areas?

Some of your organization's objectives will have a direct impact on your area of responsibility and it is likely that you are already aware of them. Some of the other objectives will not be relevant to your work and some may even be secret.

ACTIVITIES MANAGEMENT

The reality of planning

As a team leader, you operate at a level where the day-to-day work of the organization actually gets done. You will be given objectives and targets by your managers, but it is probably up to you to decide exactly how you and your team are going to achieve them. In this part of the chapter we will consider some of the practical issues you have to take into account when making plans.

How long will it take?

If you are assigning tasks to people who have performed them before, you will probably be able to make a reasonable estimate of the time the work will take. Sometimes, however, you will ask people to perform tasks with which they are not familiar.

Everyone's performance at a job improves with practice. The first time you do a task, you have to find out what needs to be done and how to do it. The second time you do a task, you will be faster. It has been calculated that, for most tasks, people improve their speed by between 80 and 90 per cent each time the number of repetitions doubles. So, if it takes one hour to do a task the first time, it will take, on average:

1 × 0.8 hours to do it the second time
1 × 0.8 × 0.8 hours to do it the fourth time
1 × 0.8 × 0.8 × 0.8 to do it the eighth time . . .

These figures can be shown on a graph (Figure 2.2):

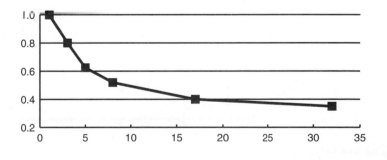

Figure 2.2

The line that you see when you join up the dots is known as a **learning curve**. As you can see, at first there is a rapid improvement in the time it takes to complete the task, but the curve quickly levels off.

PLANNING TECHNIQUES

It is important to remember that the learning curve is based on mean values and that individual performance will vary. Different tasks also have different shapes of learning curve. For example, the curve for a very difficult task will not drop so dramatically after the first few repetitions.

If you have a short task that must be repeated many times, it may be worth giving it to inexperienced individuals and allowing them time to improve their performance. If you have a longer task, which only needs to be performed once or twice, there may not be time in the schedule for an individual to move along the learning curve and it would be better to find someone more experienced to do the work.

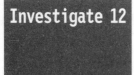

Investigate 12

Think of two tasks that are performed by your team where it would be worth allowing someone to move along the learning curve.

Think of two tasks which it would be advisable to give to a more experienced individual.

When you estimate how long a task will take, you may be tempted to base your timing on the speed at which people work when they are performing at their best. For example, if you know it is possible to complete a form in ten minutes, you may expect your staff to complete six forms every hour and forty-two forms in a seven-hour working day. However, people do not achieve peak performance all the time.

In practice, it has been found that in the first 20 per cent of time that a job takes, people work up from doing nothing to their peak rate of activity in a linear manner. The same phenomenon happens in reverse during the final 30 per cent of the time a job takes. Figure 2.3 represents what happens:

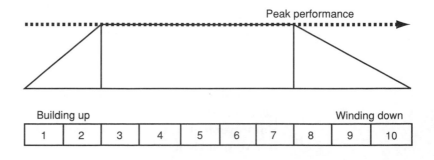

Figure 2.3

People only achieve half their peak output in the first 20 per cent and last 30 per cent of a job. Over the whole period they are working they will only achieve 75 per cent of what they could do if they were working at their most efficient rate all the time. It is more realistic to take into account the fact that people need to build up to their peak performance and will wind down at the end of a period of work.

| Investigate 13 | How long do the people in your team take to build up to (and wind down from) their peak performance? |

In Chapter 3, we will return to the subject of how people work and examine some scientific approaches to work study.

Conflicting priorities

When you make your own plans, you will have to balance different priorities – and may have to make some difficult decisions. It is likely that you will experience conflicts between the following areas of priority:

- *work* – the task that must be done to a certain standard by a particular time
- *money* – the resources that you have available and the way in which you use them
- *people* – the members of your team and your line manager.

Here are some examples:

- **a conflict between work and money**: 'My line manager told me I had to arrange interviews with all existing customers once a quarter – but she did not offer to pay for the three extra members of staff I would need to meet this target.'
- **a conflict between work and people**: 'Nobody on the team likes covering the enquiry desk at lunchtime, but it's something that has to be done.'
- **a conflict between money and people**: 'I'd love to be able to provide proper maps for the delivery team to use. It would make their lives so much easier, but I simply do not have the budget.'

As a team leader, you probably have very little control over the objectives that are set for you. You may have some leeway on how you spend your budget, but it is unlikely that you have the power to increase the total amount that is available to you. You do, however, have quite a bit of control over the people who work in your team.

Some team leaders try to resolve conflicts of priority by demanding more of the people who work for them. Others find it hard to do this. If you work alongside the members of your team, and particularly if you were once an ordinary team member yourself, you may try to resolve conflicts in other ways. For example, you may respond to all complaints about inadequate equipment by asking your line manager to increase your budget. Or you may make excuses on behalf of your team for work that has not been completed satisfactorily. There is not an easy answer to dilemmas of this kind. However, it is useful to reflect on your own preferred way of handling these conflicts – and to consider whether you always get your priorities right.

Activity 10	Think about times when you face conflicts between work, money and people. What do you usually do? In what other ways could you resolve these conflicts?

If you have a tendency to put too much (or not enough) pressure on the members of your team, this can affect the plans that you draw up. In the first situation, you may be overoptimistic about what they can achieve. In the second situation, you may not be using their full potential.

Communicating with your team

Once you have drawn up a plan, you need to communicate it to the people who will carry it out. The type and amount of information that you pass on will depend on several factors, including:

- the complexity of the task you are explaining
- how much your team knows already
- safety and security issues
- whether you want them to think about the task, or simply follow instructions.

Two popular ways of briefing people are in team meetings and in written instructions.

Team meetings

A meeting is often an appropriate way in which to introduce your team to a plan. You can save time by explaining things to everyone at once and clarify details by allowing questions and discussion. It can also be very good psychology to talk to your whole team at the same time about any new venture. People are generally suspicious of change and, if you talk to your staff individually, rumours may start to circulate amongst those who do not yet know what is going to happen.

When you prepare an agenda for a meeting, consider writing it as a series of objectives.

By the end of this meeting we will have:

1 discussed plans for the schools event to be held on 26 October
2 prepared a rota for the exhibition stand
3 drafted copy for the leaflet.

It is not usually necessary to take detailed minutes at team meetings, but it is essential that all decisions are recorded. If an individual is assigned a task, his or her name and the completion date should be written down. Before the next meeting, someone should check on progress.

Although meetings are useful when you are introducing a plan, people may also need written information about what is expected of them.

Briefing your team in writing

In general, only brief people about things they need to know. If you give them too much to read, they miss vital instructions. It is advisable to make all written instructions as short and simple as possible. There are several different ways of reminding your team of what you expect them to do. You may send round a memo to ask them to complete a particular task:

> To: all team members
>
> From: Jo Knight
>
> As discussed at last week's meeting, please make sure that you give me your completed training forms **by 4.00 p.m. on Friday 5th at the latest.**
>
> Please mark your first and second choice of course for the staff development day.

Sometimes you will want people to see how their own work relates to what others are doing. Here, a schedule may be useful:

Schedule for refurbishment of office		
7.7	Office plan completed	LP
12.7	Specifications for new furniture completed	WV
13.7	Order for new equipment placed	SA
7.8	Boxes ordered from stores	SA
13.8	Contents of filing cabinets transferred to boxes	EC, PJ
14.8	Desks cleared	ALL
14.8	IT equipment disconnected	PK
15.8/ 16.8	Contractors remove old furniture, replace with new	
17.8	Computers reconnected	PK
18.8	New filing cabinets filled	EC, PJ

A schedule can also be presented in diagrammatic form, as a Gantt chart (Figure 2.4).

Gantt charts are discussed in the final section of this chapter. When you are sending out a copy of a chart or schedule to an individual, it is useful to highlight the parts that refer specifically to him or her.

	3	4	5	6	7	8	9	10	11	12	13	14	15	16	17	18	19	20	21	22	23	24	25	26	27	28	30	1	2	3	4	5	6
Course A	●	●	●	●	●																												
Consult A								●	●																								
Revise A										●	●	●																					
Course B									●	●	●	●	●																				
Consult B															●	●																	
Revise B																	●	●	●														
Report prepared																					●	●	●	●	●								
Report presented																															●		

Figure 2.4

A checklist can be an effective method of giving instructions:

Did you remember to . . .

- ☐ pick up the telephone before it rings for a third time
- ☐ say 'This is BQM, [your first name] speaking. What can I do to help?'
- ☐ get the caller's name and number
- ☐ ask them to spell any difficult words
- ☐ tell the caller what action you are going to take
- ☐ log the call as soon as it finished

If a task can be broken down into steps that have to be performed in a particular order, a numbered list can help:

How to replace Unit XC3

1 Unscrew cap
2 Gently lift out washer
3 Clean shank, removing excess oil
4 Lift out old Unit
5 Remove new Unit from packaging
6 Give $\frac{1}{4}$ clockwise turn to ratchet screw at base of Unit
7 Lower new Unit into place
8 Replace washer
9 Replace cap
10 Recalibrate meter to zero setting
11 Dispose of old Unit and packaging

PLANNING TECHNIQUES

Activity 11 Look at some written instructions you have given to your team in the past. Present them in a different form, as a memo, a schedule, a checklist or a step-by-step guide.

Scheduling techniques

In this last section of the chapter we will examine some tools you can use to build up a schedule.

Flowcharts

A flowchart is a diagram that shows the sequence of a series of interdependent activities. When you are planning a process or event, you will often find that one activity cannot start until another has finished. For example:

- you cannot print a letter before it has been written
- you cannot plaster a wall before it has been built
- you cannot put a patient on a consultant's waiting list before he has seen his GP.

When you look at them individually, these dependencies are usually obvious. However, when you are trying to organize a complicated series of activities in which many different people or departments are involved, it is very easy to lose sight of the sequence in which things must happen.

In many processes, there are also points at which decisions have to be made. If the decision goes one way, one set of actions is taken. If it goes the other way, an alternative course is followed.

A flowchart is a way of displaying these dependencies and alternative courses of action. It consists of a series of boxes linked by arrows which show the chronological order in which activities must be completed. The shape of the boxes is also significant. By convention, these basic shapes are used:

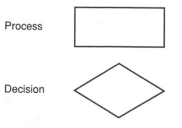

ACTIVITIES MANAGEMENT

Figure 2.5

You may also come across other shapes to indicate such things as data, storage and preparation. The following flowchart (Figure 2.6) uses the basic shapes and describes what happens when an invoice comes into the General Office of a college.

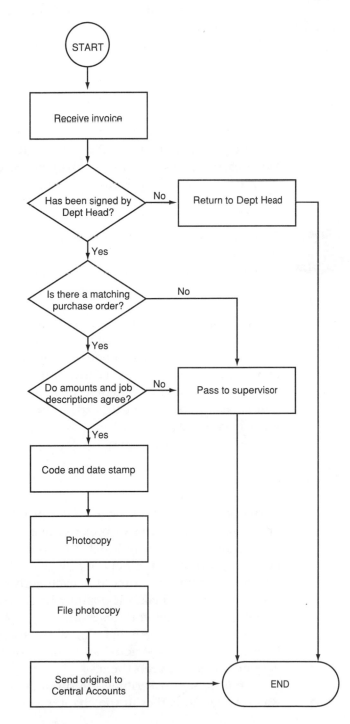

Figure 2.6

Activity 12

Study the flowchart and answer these questions.

1 In what circumstances should you send the invoice back to the Department Head?
2 In what circumstances should you pass the invoice to the supervisor?
3 Would it be possible for an uncoded invoice to be filed?

See Feedback section for answer to this activity.

A flowchart makes it easy to follow a process and think about whether it is happening in the most logical and efficient way. Flowcharts can also be used to explain a process to the people who will carry it out.

Activity 13

Draw up a flowchart for a simple process that is performed by members of your team. Can you make the process more logical or efficient?

You may find this activity more difficult than you imagine. It can sometimes be quite hard to work out the dependencies between tasks with which you are very familiar. When drawing up a flowchart, it is always best to sketch out a rough version before you try to make it look neat. Many people also find it easier to start at the end of the process and work backwards.

Network diagrams

Network diagrams work on a similar principle to flowcharts. They consist of a series of boxes connected by arrows and they show the sequence in which activities must be performed. However, a network diagram also contains information about the time that each activity will take. This extra information makes it possible to construct a detailed schedule from a network diagram.

The first stage in drawing a network diagram is to gather information about the activities to be performed and the dependencies between them.

Here is a chart describing the production of a leaflet that was referred to earlier in the chapter.

Activity number	Description	Time (days)	Dependencies
1	Write copy	4	–
2	Check copy	2	after 1
3	Design leaflet	6	after 1
4	Take photos	5	after 3
5	DTP leaflet	5	after 2 and 4
6	Check proofs	3	after 5
7	Print	5	after 6

Figure 2.7 is a network diagram of this process:

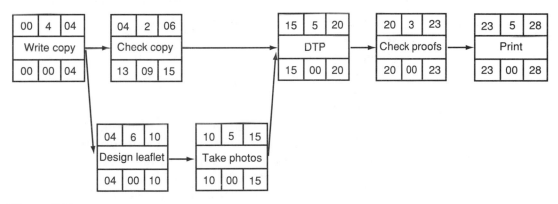

Figure 2.7

Each box in the diagram contains the following information:

Early Start	Duration	Early Finish
Task name		
Late Start	Slack	Late Finish

Figure 2.8

The Early Start time is the earliest that an activity can begin. The Early Finish time is the earliest time that it can end. Similarly, the Late Start and Late Finish times are the latest times that the activity can begin and end. The Duration is the time that the activity will take. In this diagram, it is given in days; in other situations, it could be given in months, weeks or even hours. The Slack is any extra time that is available for an activity. You may have heard the term **critical path**, or **critical path analysis**. The critical path is the route through the diagram that connects activities that do not have any slack. If these activities are delayed, the whole process is held up. It is useful to identify the critical path, because this tells you where you need to concentrate your effort and resources at any time.

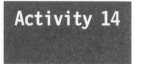

Which tasks lie on the critical path in the network diagram shown here?

See Feedback section for answer to this activity.

How to draw up a network diagram

1 Start by sketching out the boxes. Each activity needs a box. Use arrows to show which tasks are dependent on each other.
2 Name the tasks.
3 Starting at the left-hand side of the diagram, fill in the earliest time an activity can start, and its duration.
4 Add the duration to the Early Start time and work out the earliest time the activity can finish.
5 Move on to the next box and do the same. The earliest start time is always the same as the earliest finish time in the preceding box. If two boxes lead into one, select the later time.
6 When you have reached the box at the right of the diagram, copy the figure for the Early Finish time into the Late Finish time.
7 Now work backward through the diagram, using the durations to fill in the Late Finish time and the Late Start time in each box. The Late Finish time is the same as the Late Start time in the box connected by an arrow on the right. If you have two latest start times, select the earlier time.
8 Finally, fill in the slack time by subtracting the Early Finish time from the Late Finish time in each box. If these figures are identical, there is no slack.

Activity 15

Draw a network diagram for a simple process that you are responsible for at work.

In order to explain the principles of network diagrams, we chose a very simple process for our example. It would not normally be worth going to the trouble of drawing up a diagram for a process of this kind. However, if you are trying to plan a complicated series of activities, network diagrams can be useful.

Gantt charts

Gantt charts are a simple, but very effective, method of representing a plan. They can be drawn by hand, presented on specially designed wallcharts with magnetic or adhesive strips, or prepared on a computer. The basic framework is a chart in which time is measured along the horizontal scale and activities are listed vertically.

This Gantt chart (Figure 2.9) shows the production of the leaflet. Each column represents one day. They are numbered sequentially. Notice that the activity 'check copy' is going on at the same time as the leaflet is being designed.

	1	2	3	4	5	6	7	8	9	10	11	12	13	14	15	16	17	18	19	20	21	22	23	24	25	26	27	28
Write copy	■	■	■	■																								
Check copy					■	■																						
Design leaflet					■	■	■	■	■	■	■																	
Take photos												■	■	■	■	■												
DTP																■	■	■	■									
Check proofs																				■	■	■						
Print																							■	■	■	■	■	■

Figure 2.9

Before you draw up a Gantt chart, you need to work out:

- the tasks that must be performed
- the order in which they need to happen
- the duration of each task.

	16	17	18	19	20			23	24	25	26	27			30	31	1	2	3			6	7	8	9	10			13	14	15	16	17			20	21	22	23
Write copy																																							
Check copy																																							
Design leaflet																																							
Take photos																																							
DTP																																							
Check proofs																																							
Print																																							

Figure 2.10

It is often helpful to draw up a chart, like the one that was used to gather information for the network diagram. If you are not sure about the dependencies between the tasks, you may like to draw up a flowchart as well.

You can very easily convert a Gantt chart into a schedule that everyone can understand. In Figure 2.10, the figures at the top have been replaced by dates. Weekends have also been inserted, to give a clearer impression of when exactly tasks have to be done.

The dates in this schedule are based on the understanding that everyone will complete their tasks in the expected time. In real life, this does not always happen. It is always advisable to add some extra time into the schedule to allow for delays. You can:

• add a little time to every activity
• add time to those activities you think may take longer
• keep the extra time for the end of the schedule and tell people you need everything finished on a date some time in advance of the real deadline.

In some situations, you might also have to add extra time for postage or delivery.

<table>
<tr><td>**Activity 16**</td><td>Draw a Gantt chart for the process you showed earlier in a network diagram.</td></tr>
</table>

Summary

The planning process follows essentially the same pattern, whether it takes place on an organizational or personal scale. After identifying your goal, you should clarify your present position and consider the range of strategies you could use to get from where you are to where you want to be. You then select the most appropriate strategy and break it down into smaller steps. Drawing up a plan is only the first stage in the planning cycle. You must then implement your plan, monitor it and then evaluate it.

In an organization, the planning process starts with a mission statement that sets the general direction. The plan is then developed in greater levels of detail by managers at various levels within the organization. Senior managers work out long-term strategic plans; middle managers are concerned with medium-term operational plans and junior managers make short-term action plans.

Managers use a range of tools to help them plan, including an examination of the STEP factors in the outside environment and a SWOT analysis of the organization's position. They also use forecasting techniques to try to predict the future financial position. Objectives, which should be SMART, are important at all levels of management.

When you are estimating how much work your team will actually be able to achieve, you should be aware that people do not achieve peak performance all the time. It also takes people some time to learn new tasks. There are several techniques you can use to communicate your plans to your team, including written memos, meetings, schedules, checklists and Gantt charts.

The dependencies between different tasks can be worked out using a flowchart. Scheduled dates can then be set, using a network diagram or a Gantt chart.

Review and discussion questions

1 What are the four stages of the planning cycle?
2 What four elements does a mission statement normally contain?
3 What do these initials stand for?
   a STEP
   b SMART
   c SWOT
4 What factors should you take into account when you decide how you will communicate your plans to your team?
5 What is the significance of the critical path in a network diagram?

Case study

As a result of a quality initiative within a college, it was decided that something needed to be done to improve the induction of new students. The team leader in charge of Student Services was asked to commission a short video and an explanatory leaflet. The video is to be produced by media students at the start of the summer vacation. The leaflet is to include stills from the video.

The team leader talked to everyone involved and gathered the following information:

• 'It will take two weeks to shoot the video and another two weeks to edit it.'

- 'I'll write the leaflet for you. I could do it in a week sometime in August. I'll have to send it to the Principal to get the copy checked out.'
- 'Allow a week for design and layout of the leaflet.'
- 'It's only a day's work to put stills from the video into the leaflet.'
- 'The college printshop can print copies off in three days. They are working throughout August.'
- 'The Principal ought to see the script for the video and the final copy. He's around all summer, but you ought to allow a week for him to check things out.'

Use this information to prepare a schedule for the video and the leaflet.

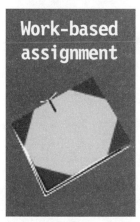

Work-based assignment

Draw up a plan that you could use to improve some aspect of your team's activities. Your plan should be realistic and based upon your team's objectives. Prepare the documents you would use to communicate the plan to the team.

Action plan

This action plan can be used to prepare for a meeting at which you will discuss a plan that will affect the work of your team.

1 Decide your objectives for the meeting.
2 Identify staff who should attend the meeting.
3 If necessary, book the room.
4 Inform staff of the meeting.
5 Identify information that staff will need from you at the meeting.
6 Write the agenda.
7 Appoint a scribe for the meeting.
8 Prepare documents for the meeting.
9 Hold the meeting.

PLANNING TECHNIQUES

3 Monitoring activities

Learning objectives

On completion of this chapter you will be able to:

- select appropriate indicators for monitoring activities
- choose an appropriate method of monitoring activities
- obtain and provide quality information for monitoring purposes
- apply a problem-solving technique
- recognize and solve problems brought about by the personalities of team members
- update your plans where necessary
- manage changes to your plans effectively
- describe work study techniques
- recommend improvements to working processes.

NVQ links

This chapter covers underpinning knowledge required for the vocational qualification in management at level 3 for the mandatory unit:

Unit A1 Maintain activities to meet requirements

A1.1 Maintain work activities to meet requirements
A1.2 Maintain healthy, safe and productive working conditions
A1.3 Make recommendations for improvements to work activities

Introduction

After you have drawn up your plans and put them into action, you need to monitor what happens. This is the third stage of the planning cycle – and the stage at which things are most likely to go wrong.

ACTIVITIES MANAGEMENT

There are several ways in which plans can go off course:

- people do not do the right things
- people do the right things at the wrong time
- people do the right things, but these things have the wrong effect
- unexpected events intervene.

Imagine you have made a plan for a celebration lunch in the office. Here are some examples of things that could go wrong:

- *people do not do the right things* – someone forgets to set out the tables in the room where you are holding the lunch
- *people do the right things at the wrong time* – the caterers are late in arriving with the food
- *people do the right things, but these things have the wrong effect* – the Chief Executive turns up to make a speech as arranged, but what he says upsets several of the guests
- *unexpected events intervene* – half an hour before the lunch is supposed to begin the fire alarm goes off and the building has to be evacuated.

It is relatively easy to guard against the first two types of event. If you have a clear description of what is supposed to happen at particular times, whether it is in the form of a schedule, a budget forecast or a simple list, you can check that pre-planned tasks are performed at the appropriate moment. However, you must also monitor whether your plan is having the desired effect. If, like the Chief Executive's unfortunate speech, it has unexpected consequences, you may have to deviate from your plan. You may have to make new arrangements, for example, by asking another senior member of staff to go round and smooth the ruffled feathers of the people who have been upset. In the monitoring phase, you may also have to cope with completely unexpected events. Here, you may have to make new arrangements very quickly. The ease with which you do this will depend on:

- the seriousness of the intervening event
- how much extra money and time you have built into your budgets and schedules
- the amount of thought you have given to contingency plans.

MONITORING ACTIVITIES

Monitoring activities is not simply a matter of checking tasks off on a list. It demands an understanding of what you are actually trying to achieve, flexibility and the ability to think on your feet. In this chapter we will examine techniques that you can use to maintain control over events as they unfold.

The monitoring function

There are two distinct types of activities that you may have to monitor at work. If you are monitoring ongoing operations, such as, for example, the day-to-day functioning of a help desk, the processing of invoices before they go to the accounts department or the manufacture of components on an assembly line, your main concern is stability. You know, from past records and experience, what is supposed to happen. You also know what resources are necessary in order for these processes to happen. In your monitoring, you need to focus on unusual events. These anomalies can come to your notice at the input or output stage of the operation, or during the process itself. (These three stages are described in Figure 1.1 on page 7.)

Activity 17

Would you categorize the following as problems discovered at the input, process or output stage?

1 One of the two people who staff the help desk does not turn up for work.
2 Your line manager telephones to say that a client has complained that the components he has bought are 2 mm too large.
3 The only photocopier in the building breaks down while someone is copying some documents to be handed out at an important meeting.

See Feedback section for answer to this activity.

Investigate 14

Think about an operation that you are responsible for. What problems or difficulties should you watch out for at the input, process and output stages?

The second type of activity for which you may make plans is a project. Project management is different from operational management because projects are, by definition, unique. Although a project may have some similarities with other projects that have happened in the past, it will also have some significant differences. A project also has a beginning, a middle and an end. It is not a continuous process. For these reasons, the idea of stability that is so important when you are monitoring ongoing operations is not particularly helpful when you are monitoring a project. Instead, it is more useful to focus on the objectives that you need to achieve at each stage.

What do you need to monitor?

Every activity can be broken down into a series of tasks. A task is something that has a definite start and finish and takes a measurable amount of cost, effort, resources and time. A task also results in an end-product that can be checked.

Imagine that you have been asked to supervise the sending of 1000 mailshots to customers. You plan to organize it like this:

1 order special envelopes from local stationers
2 select appropriate group of customers from the database
3 ask reprographics to print 1000 copies of a letter supplied to you by the Marketing Department
4 print the addresses on the envelopes
5 fold the letters by hand and insert them into the envelopes
6 put the letters through the automatic franking machine
7 take the letters to the Post Office.

Activity 18

What end-product would you need to check for each of these tasks? What kinds of check would you make?

See Feedback section for answer to this activity.

Your answers to this activity may not be exactly the same as ours, but you probably identified several different kinds of check that you would make. Generally, there are three aspects of activities that you need to monitor:

• time
• money
• quality.

Monitoring time

You may have to monitor the time at which a task begins and the time at which it is completed. If the task is a long one, or is particularly important, it may also be advisable to check progress while the task is underway, making sure that it is proceeding at the rate you expected.

Monitoring money

Depending on the type of work that you are monitoring, you may have to check the money that is spent, the money that is received, or both. In many business situations, there is frequently a time lag between the date at which payment is requested and the date at which the cash actually changes hands. This delay can be extremely significant. For example, a company that has just issued a large number of invoices can appear, on paper, to be in a very healthy position. However, it could actually be in severe cash flow difficulties until the cash is received.

Investigate 15

What responsibilities do you have for monitoring money? At what point do you monitor payments and income? Does this system give you an accurate picture of the situation?

Monitoring quality

This involves checking that the output matches the specifications that have been set. It may also be necessary to find out whether the output meets the requirements of the customer. For example, if you were monitoring a training course that was being organized by outside consultants, you would need to check that:

- the consultants deliver the kind of course they had promised (checking against specifications)
- the trainees benefit from the course (checking that customers' requirements are met).

In many situations, it can be useful to get the reactions of customers before you commit all your resources to an activity. For example, in the situation discussed in the previous activity, the marketing department may have sent its letter to a few sample customers before ordering the full mail shot.

How much do you need to monitor?

When you delegate work to other people, it can be tempting to try to monitor every detail of what they are doing. This is a waste of your time and can also be seriously counterproductive. If the people who are doing the work have appropriate skills and experience, and you have briefed them properly, then they should be quite capable of working without constant checking. If you monitor them too closely, you may distract them from what they are doing. They may also suspect that you do not trust them to complete the task. This will lower their morale and they may even start making deliberate errors, just to see how carefully you are watching them.

It is usually much more effective to give people more autonomy in their work and take on the role of a facilitator and adviser, only stepping in when they get into difficulties. You do not have to justify your existence by the complexity of your routine monitoring system. It is more important to direct your attention towards non-routine events. You can be much more useful as a problem-solver, a mediator and a motivator than as a time-keeper. A good monitoring system will:

- run smoothly and efficiently with the minimum of effort
- allow you to see the overall implications of what is happening
- highlight anomalies and significant developments immediately
- free up your time so that you can concentrate your efforts on areas that really need your attention.

In any activity, there are some areas that are more important than others. In Chapter 2 you looked at network diagrams and saw that the tasks that lie on the critical path are those that could hold up the whole process if they are delayed. It is worth monitoring these tasks more closely than others, whose timing is less crucial.

Before an organization funds a major new project, it will probably perform an exercise known as a **sensitivity analysis**. This involves taking each item on a budget forecast

MONITORING ACTIVITIES

and calculating the percentage by which that figure would have to change to make the total cash inflow from the project less than the cash outflow. In so doing, it highlights the critical figures on the budget forecast. These are figures that need to be watched particularly carefully during the monitoring phase. For example, the success of a project with a high labour content might depend on the wages paid to casual staff not exceeding the budgeted figure by more than 5 per cent. If you noticed a 4 per cent drop in the work rate, or a 4 per cent rise in the wage bill, this would be a serious cause for concern. On the other hand, the cost of raw materials might be able to rise by 30 per cent before it affected the profitability of the project. A 4 per cent rise in the cost of raw materials would therefore be a relatively unimportant matter.

Investigate 16

Think about a project you have been involved in at work. What were the really crucial figures that were essential to the project's success?

Prices can be just as important as costs. If the amount that a business can expect to receive for its products suddenly drops, it may have to reformulate its plans.

There may also be critical issues in relation to quality that demand your special attention. These can involve legal issues and anything related to the health and safety of customers, the workforce and the general public. Here are some examples:

> Furniture manufacturer: 'We state in our sales literature that all our furniture is made from sustainable hardwoods. That means that we have to be especially careful in our choice of suppliers. We demand much more information than most manufacturers about where the timber has come from.'

> Contract cleaner: 'We obviously check all the floors and landings for litter, but we take extra care that nothing has been dropped on the stairs, where it could cause an accident.'

> Hospital administrator: 'We could be sued by patients if their medical records fell into the wrong hands, so we operate a strict security system on the computers.'

How do you monitor activities?

There is a wide variety of methods you can use to monitor the activities of your team.

Self-monitoring

If the members of your team have a full understanding of what they are doing and a commitment to quality, there will be many tasks that they can monitor for themselves.

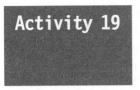

List some situations where you would definitely allow your team members to monitor themselves – and some situations that you would definitely need to monitor yourself.

See Feedback section for answer to this activity.

Automatic monitoring

Many aspects of work can now be monitored automatically. Examples include:

- sales on an electronic till
- the distance travelled in a lorry and recorded on the tachograph
- calls made on a telephone
- the time spent working on a text document or a database on a computer.

Modern technology can record a tremendous amount of data with very little human effort being necessary. When it is analysed, this data can yield interesting information. However, the process of analysis and interpretation takes time. It is not worth gathering large amounts of data if you will never look at it again. Some team members may also feel threatened if they are electronically monitored. This is not necessarily an indication that they are trying to cheat the organization – they may simply not want other people to know exactly how they work.

Meetings

Meetings are a popular way of monitoring the activity of a team, especially if it is involved in project or non-routine work. Team meetings can be a good way to let everyone know what the rest of the team is doing and to increase motivation. However, they should not be held simply to discuss routine activity. Meetings should not usually be used to report events which could just as easily be communicated on paper, by telephone or by electronic mail. Also, if you are having difficulties with a particular individual on your team, or a specific technical process is causing problems, a team meeting is probably not the right situation in which to sort things out.

Team meetings should only be held if there are non-routine matters of interest and relevance to the majority of the team that need discussion. If written reports are submitted in advance of a meeting, this can provide a useful stimulus for people to get their records up-to-date and settle outstanding issues.

Investigate 17

What did you discuss at your last team meeting? How much of the agenda was relevant to each of the people present?

Informal contacts

You probably gain most information about what your team is doing by walking round and talking to them as they work. This should not feel like a tour of inspection, but an opportunity for people to bring up any problems they are having. If team members do not see your presence as a threat, they are less likely to hide things from you. As well as having regular day-to-day contact with your team, you should also give people the chance to talk to you privately if they have difficulties that they do not want the rest of the team to know about.

Activity 20

Do your team members tell you if they are having difficulties with their work?

Do they tell you if they are having personal difficulties, such as illness or family trouble, that is affecting their work?

If you answered no to either of these questions, you may need to consider *why* your team members do not give you this information. Perhaps you intimidate your team. Perhaps you do not encourage them to talk to you. Or perhaps you work in an environment where it is impossible to have a private conversation. You may also find it easier to talk to some of the people in your team than others. While people are entitled to a certain amount of privacy at work, and you definitely do not need to know about every detail of their lives, it is important that you keep channels of communication open, so that you hear about any difficulties before they become crises.

Reports

Reports on progress are frequently delivered in preset formats, as forms or charts. This is a way of ensuring that all the necessary information is included. Reports can be given on issues related to money, time and quality.

As a team leader, you are likely to have to complete some form of budget report. The example on the next page records sales in a particular month. In the left-hand column, the items included in the report are listed. The next column of headings lists the volume of sales, the price at which sales were made and the value of the sales. It would be possible simply to record the value of sales from each item in a month, but this would not tell managers whether any difference between the estimated and actual figures was due to a change in price or a change in the volume of sales.

On the right of the report there are three columns. The first of these gives the estimated figures that were provided before the budget period covered by the report began. The manager who is asked to complete the report may have come up with these figures him or herself on an earlier occasion, or they may have been supplied by another department. The manager who completes this report may be asked to provide updated estimates for next month's budget, or the estimates may be updated centrally.

The actual column records the number, volume and price of sales that have actually been made. To avoid confusion, there must be a clear policy in the organization about the point at which sales are recorded. This is likely to be when an invoice is issued.

The final column records the variance between the estimated and actual figures. This can be a plus or minus figure.

MONITORING ACTIVITIES

SALES BUDGET 1998		Month: June		
		Est	Act	Var
Model A	Volume	2000	2321	+321
	Price	5.00	5.00	0
	Value	10 000.00	11 605.00	+1605.00
Model C1	Volume	230	198	−32
	Price	15.00	15.00	0
	Value	3450.00	2970.00	−480.00
Model 222	Volume	900	890	−10
	Price	3.00	4.00	+33%
	Value	2700.00	3560.00	+860.00
Model 404	Volume	875	997	+122
	Price	7.95	7.95	0
	Value	6956.25	7926.15	+969.90

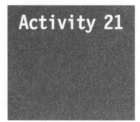

Activity 21

Study the sales report.

1 How many more (or less) items has the company sold than expected?
2 How much more (or less) money have sales brought in than expected?

See Feedback section for answer to this activity.

The example here was a sales report. The same basic structure, with estimated, actual and variance figures given for a list of separate items, can be used for other types of budget, too.

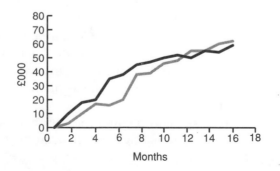

Figure 3.1

Financial information can also be displayed in graph form, like the example here (Figure 3.1). Graphs give a quick general impression of the situation, but they usually need to be accompanied by tables that give the exact figures.

Activity 22

Study Figure 3.1 carefully. It shows the cumulative amount of money that an organization expected to spend on a project and the cumulative actual spending.

1 Do you think the project is proving more or less expensive than expected?
2 Do you think the project is up to schedule?

See Feedback section for answer to this activity.

If you are managing a project, you will probably have to report on the schedule. Your report should list the dates at which events were supposed to have happened and the dates at which they actually happened, if they are different. Your report may look something like this document, which is based on the schedule you looked at in Chapter 2:

Schedule for leaflet

Action		Scheduled date	Actual date
1 Write copy	CM	20.8	20.8
2 Copy checked for accuracy	RR	22.8	24.8
3 Leaflet designed	EWL	30.8	31.8
4 Photographs taken	EWL	6.9	8.9
5 Desktop publishing of leaflet	EWL	13.9	14.9
6 Proofs checked	RR, CM	16.9	16.9
7 Leaflet printed	TT	23.9	23.9

The right-hand column is used to record the dates at which the stages actually took place.

In many situations you will also need to monitor the quality of the work you are managing. In a project, task sheets may be completed and signed off as each element is finished and checked. If the specifications are not met exactly, this should be noted. It is usual to link quality checks with authorization for payment. This ensures that money is not spent on sub-standard work and is a great incentive for staff or departments who are paid in this way to expedite any documentation.

As well as recording estimated and actual data relating to money, time and quality, you will also need to explain any variance, slippage or departure from specifications. You may have to give this report verbally, or in writing. Your line managers will be interested in knowing *why* things have not gone to plan, and whether there are likely to be any wider implications. You want your managers to think that you are in control of the situation and it can be very tempting to try to minimize any difficulties when you are reporting on progress. However, if you are genuinely worried about your ability to meet any aspect of the budget, schedule or specifications, it is a good idea to alert your managers as soon as possible. This is much better than surprising them with a critical situation at a later date, when it is too late to put things right.

Information for monitoring

You need quality information if you are going to make effective decisions. The information that you gather for monitoring purposes should be:

- relevant
- adequate
- up-to-date
- reliable.

It is important that the information you obtain is relevant to the issues you need to monitor. The system you use to gather information should be based on the same structure, and use the same categories, as you used at the planning stage. This makes it much easier to see how your plans are working out in practice.

The information you gather needs to be adequate for the way in which you are going to use it. Think about how much detail you really need. You should avoid collecting irrelevant or unnecessary information. Do not waste your own time (and the time of other people) gathering, processing and storing any information which will not be of use to you. If you ask for too much information, you may distract your team from the work they are supposed to be doing. Also, if you are overloaded with information to look at and analyse, you may lose focus on the really important issues. These effects can actually outweigh any benefits you receive from building up a large database of information for future analysis.

Information has a limited useful life. The information you gather for monitoring purposes needs to be up-to-date. This means that it should be collected at appropriate intervals. The frequency of these intervals will depend on the activities involved and the degree of control you need to exert. When a new operation is just beginning, you may need to check more frequently than you do later on, when your team is more familiar with the task. You also need to select a method for collecting information that allows you to see it as soon as possible. The channel of communication (telephone, internal post, fax, e-mail, meetings, etc.) can be very important here. You should also try to avoid the need to spend unnecessary time compiling and analysing data, if this can be done automatically.

Finally, information needs to be reliable. You have to be able to trust the information you receive. As far as possible, you should ask for information that people are willing to give you. If you ask your team to report on things that will incriminate themselves, or other people, they may not be entirely honest with you. You should also always ask people questions that they are *able* to answer. If you ask impossible questions, they may provide you with worthless answers. This can sometimes happen if you ask people to make projections about the future or to speculate about issues where they do not have sufficient knowledge.

Wherever possible, you should ask for information which is verifiable. If your team know that you can check up on what they tell you, they are more likely to be accurate. Your monitoring system should have built-in checks.

Investigate 18

Consider the information you gather from your team to monitor activities. Is it relevant, adequate, up-to-date and reliable? In what ways could it be improved?

Also consider the information you pass to your own manager about your team's activities. Is this information relevant, adequate, up-to-date and reliable? In what ways could it be improved?

Problem solving

It is inevitable that, from time to time, your monitoring activities will reveal that things are not going exactly to plan. In this part of the chapter we will examine some methods of dealing with problems.

How to solve problems

When a plan goes wrong, it can be difficult to keep a clear head. Some people do nothing, hoping that the problem will go away. Others act too quickly, implementing the first solution that comes to mind, and may sometimes make the problem worse. However, many managers use a more logical approach to problem solving.

Step 1: define the boundaries of the problem.
Step 2: identify the cause of the problem.
Step 3: think of a range of ways of solving the problem.
Step 4: choose the most appropriate solution.

Begin by thinking about how extensive the problem really is. You can ask questions like these:

• When did the problem start?
• Who is involved?
• How much is it costing us?
• Does it happen all the time?
• What would happen if we did nothing?

Quite often, a problem that appears to be extremely significant can dramatically reduce in importance if you examine it calmly in this way. Here are two examples:

My line manager came to me and said that she'd had a memo from the supervisor in the warehouse saying they were unable to handle our orders any longer. I went down to investigate. It turned out that the head of warehouse staff had got upset because on two occasions a large order had been sent from our department without the necessary codes being filled in. The orders had been sent down by two different members of staff. The orders were correct, it was just that a reference number had been missed out and this meant that the orders were delayed while someone in the warehouse got the necessary information. That's all it was. I apologized and, of course, I didn't make it obvious to the warehouse supervisor that I thought the problem was trivial.

My assistant said that several members of the team were threatening to hand in their notice. They were apparently very unhappy about a new rota system and did not want to implement it. The system was something that I had devised myself to try to extend our opening hours. Instead of everyone working from 9 a.m. to 5 p.m., I wanted some staff to come in at 8 a.m. and leave at 4 p.m. while others would work from 10 a.m. to 6 p.m.. I brought the subject up at a team meeting. It turned out that seventeen of the twenty people on the team thought my idea was a good one. However, there were three members of the team who would find it difficult to get in at the new time because they had to get their children off to school before they could leave for work.

Problems can sometimes be exaggerated by staff who are under pressure themselves or who have a particular view about you or your department.

Once you have isolated where exactly the problem lies, you should consider the causes. If you remember the Fishbone diagram (Figure 3.1) described in Chapter 1, you may recall that the causes of most problems are due to:

- people
- processes
- materials
- equipment.

Activity 23

How would you describe the causes of the two problems described above?

1 the warehouse problem
2 the rota problem.

See Feedback section for answer to this activity.

MONITORING ACTIVITIES

The next step is to think of ways of solving the problem. There is usually more than one solution possible. For example, in the warehouse problem, you could:

- explain the process again to the two members of your team who had made the mistake
- send a memo to all members of the team reminding them of the process
- take these individuals down to the warehouse and let the supervisor explain the system
- go through the process with everyone at a team meeting.

The final step is to choose the best solution. Here is what the team leader decided to do in this situation:

> *Two separate members of staff had made this mistake, so I thought there might be some confusion about the process amongst the team generally. I decided to spend a little time at the next team meeting reminding everyone what they were supposed to do. I thought that was better than sending a memo round because it gave people a chance to ask questions. I didn't want to involve the warehouse supervisor, because he was likely to be quite rude to the people who had made the mistake.*

Activity 24

What solutions can you think of for the rota problem? Which solution would you choose?

See Feedback section for answer to this activity.

People problems

As a team leader, you are likely to find that a large proportion of the problems you face are caused by the people you are trying to manage. This may be because you are asking individuals to take on roles to which they are not naturally suited, or because certain personalities on your team seem to clash. It can help to think about the different types of team personality that were identified by Belbin.

The **plant** is a creative individual who makes his or her own rules. A plant can find imaginative solutions to problems, but is impatient about working out the details. This person may be way ahead of other members of the team and can find it difficult to communicate with them.

The **resource investigator** is very energetic, especially at the beginning of a project. He or she is a good communicator. However, the resource investigator tends to lose interest once things are underway.

The **co-ordinator** is skilled at chairing meetings and can help people make sensible decisions. The main strength of the co-ordinator is in assisting other team members to work effectively.

The **shaper** is a dynamic individual who can set the pace for other people to follow. He or she works best when under pressure. However, the shaper may be insensitive to the feelings of other people and may need to be kept in check at times.

The **monitor evaluator** weighs up the situation carefully and comes to considered judgements. Because the monitor evaluator has high standards, he or she may be very critical of other people's work. The monitor evaluator is not a good source of creative ideas and is unlikely to inspire other people.

The **teamworker** is happy to work as a member of a team. He or she will listen to other people's points of view and work constructively alongside them. The teamworker hates arguments and will do everything possible to avoid them. This can sometimes be a weakness. However, if you have other, more assertive personalities on your team, the teamworker can be a calming influence. The teamworker is not a natural leader and can find it hard to make decisions. He or she may be overly influenced by other people.

The **implementer** is the reliable and efficient individual who actually turns ideas into reality. The implementer is usually highly skilled in a particular area. However, he or she may be rather inflexible and unwilling to adopt new ideas. The implementer may be rather quiet and may be underestimated by other members of the team.

The **completer** is an extremely conscientious person who can be relied on to follow up details. He or she often worries about the work and finds it difficult to delegate. Other members of the team can find the completer's obsessive attention to detail rather irritating.

The specialist has a great deal of technical knowledge in a particular (and often rather narrow) area. The specialist is much more interested in his or her own work than in what the rest of the team is doing.

These personality types can work well together, complementing each others' strengths and weaknesses. However, some problems can also occur. For example:

- the shaper and the plant can offend the completer and the implementer
- the monitor evaluator can find it difficult to get along with the shaper
- the teamworker can hold things up by his or her inability to make decisions
- the specialist may ignore the rules you set for the team
- the co-ordinator may be good at organizing other people, but not be able to contribute much else to the work of the team.

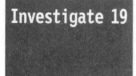

Investigate 19

Think about the people in your team. Which of Belbin's personality types do they each resemble most? What problems could be caused by the combination of personalities you have on your team? What could you do to avoid these problems?

If you know the individuals on your team well, you can try to put them in situations where their strengths will be of most value and their weaknesses will do least damage. You can also encourage them to develop the skills they find difficult. For example, you might have to help a completer to manage his or her time more efficiently. Or you might help an implementer to become more assertive.

Updating your plans

However carefully you have drawn up your plans, you may have to make some changes when you actually carry them out. If your monitoring reveals that you are not going to achieve your objectives by using your resources in the way you planned, you have four basic options:

1 make use of any contingency in your schedule or budget
2 use your resources in a different way
3 bring in more resources
4 change your objectives.

Using your contingency allowance

Your budget should have some extra money included for unforeseen contingencies. You should also have some slack time built into your schedule. These allowances can be used if there is no other way of meeting your objectives. However, it is important to remember that they can only be used once. It is dangerous to use up all these contingency allowances in the early stages of a project, because you may be in even greater difficulties later on.

Use your resources in a different way

You may be able to deploy your resources in a slightly different way. Here are some examples:

I ran out of money when I was upgrading the computer equipment in the department. Instead of buying a stand-alone fax machine, I invested in a fax modem for the computer.

It turned out that the trainee I had taken on as an administrator was not very good at answering the telephone. But she was very skilled at word processing. With the agreement of the people concerned, I arranged for the office junior to deal with the telephone, which she enjoyed, and got the administrator to deal with the documents that the department produced.

Our weekly team meetings were a waste of time. Everyone had to stop their work for an hour and often very little was achieved. I decided to use the time in a different way by sending out a twice weekly e-mail to all staff, telling them of developments they needed to be aware of. We only had a team meeting when there was a topic that we needed to discuss.

Using your resources in a different way often requires creative thinking. If you have always used a particular budget in a certain way, you may find it hard to imagine any alternatives. It can be helpful to get the views of other people, who do not share your preconceptions, on what you could do.

Identify an area of work where you find it difficult to achieve your objectives. At a team meeting, brainstorm the problem. What other solutions can people come up with?

Fast tracking

If you are short of time to complete your schedule, you may be able to use a technique known as **fast tracking** to achieve your objectives. Figure 3.2 represents a process that is made up of six separate tasks. This is the kind of schedule you may see when an item is worked on by a succession of individuals with different skills. As soon as the first task has finished, the second task can begin. And as soon as the second task is completed, the third task can start, and so on. Each task takes a week to complete. The whole process will therefore take six weeks.

Figure 3.2

Task 1						
Task 2						
Task 3						
Task 4						
Task 5						
Task 6						

Figure 3.3

Task 1						
Task 2						
Task 3						
Task 4						
Task 5						
Task 6						

Figure 3.3 shows what happens when the process is fast tracked. Each task has been split into three parts, each of which will take one-third of a week to complete. As soon as the first part of the first task is completed, the second task is started. Instead of taking six weeks, the process now takes less than three weeks.

This is a significant saving of time. However, fast tracking does have some disadvantages. If something goes wrong in the later stages of any of the tasks, subsequent work may be wasted. Imagine that the process shown here is the preparation of a catalogue. The first task is the writing of the copy. The first few pages are written and passed to the designer (task 2). As soon as the designer has planned these pages, the photographer is commissioned to take the photographs (task 3). This could all happen in the first week. But on Friday afternoon, the copywriter, who is just completing the last pages, realizes that he has written far too much and must go back and reduce the length of the product descriptions throughout the catalogue. This means that the time that designer has spent planning the pages is wasted. And the photographer, who has already begun work on the first section, may also have wasted his time. Fast tracking is dangerous in any situation where there is any degree of uncertainty about what needs to be done.

Bringing in more resources

You may be able to bring in more people, or more equipment, to complete a job. If it takes one operative six hours to do a job, three people could do the same job in two hours.

Activity 25	What are the potential disadvantages of bringing in more people to complete a task?

See Feedback section for answer to this activity.

If you have to bring in more resources, you will probably have to increase your budget. You can only do this with the consent of your manager. You will need to convince him or her that the extra resources really are necessary. Your manager will decide whether the time, cost or quality of the final product is most important and will make the decision accordingly.

Changing your objectives

You should only change your objectives as a last resort – and only after you have obtained the agreement of your manager or the internal or external customer who is going to receive your product or service. You may be able to negotiate a reduction in the specification, a delayed delivery date or an increased price. Whenever possible, you should allow the other people involved say which of these options they prefer. Do not change your objectives until you have considered all the other ways of updating your plans.

Change control

When plans are changed, you need to take great care to ensure that everyone is aware of what is going to happen. Change in any area can have serious implications for other areas of work, some of which you may not understand fully yourself.

> *I cancelled a meeting because we had a crisis in the office. I didn't realize that the person I was going to see was off on holiday for three weeks that evening, so I missed the chance to talk to her.*

> *I tried to save money by purchasing equipment from a different supplier whose prices were much lower. I didn't realize that the specifications were lower, too. The new equipment ended up costing us a lot extra.*

In a project, change control must be organized properly. Information is gathered on any changes that occur, or are likely to occur. This information must be passed swiftly to a central control point. The person who is leading the project must consider possible implications, discussing them with people who have specialist knowledge of particular areas. One way to gather information on the effect of changes to the project plan is to issue an **Impact Analysis Form**. This document is circulated to anyone who is likely to be affected by a change. It asks for the following information:

- What activities will be affected?
- Will any extra activities be necessary?
- Will these activities take longer, or be delayed?
- Is there any impact on the resources needed?
- Will the specification be affected?

Once a change has been agreed, everyone who is affected must be informed. All changes to schedules, specifications or budgets should be communicated in a recognized format, not simply passed on by word of mouth. If you are distributing revised versions of any documents, you should make it clear that these versions supersede any versions that are currently in circulation.

Investigate 21 Look around your office. Check the briefing papers and guidelines that are used by your team. Is anybody working with out-dated versions?

When you issue a revised version of a document, it is a good idea to ask people to destroy the old version. Put a date on the documents you send to your team and remind them which version they should be using.

Recommending improvements

In the final phase of the planning cycle, you should evaluate your plans. If you are working on a project, this evaluation comes at the end, when you have delivered whatever it was that you were working on. You need to evaluate:

- whether the objectives of the project have been met
- whether you could make any improvements if you organized a similar project in the future.

Meeting the objectives of a project

If you have been working towards clear objectives, it should be a relatively easy matter to check whether you have met them. Ask yourself:

- Did I meet the specifications?
- Was I on time?
- Did I achieve these results within my budget?

When you deliver your final product, your internal or external customer may be delighted with what you have achieved. However, even though you may have delivered exactly what you promised at the beginning of the project, your customer may still not be satisfied. This can happen if there was something wrong with the original objectives. In this situation, it is important to know where things went wrong,

MONITORING ACTIVITIES

even if you were not personally responsible for setting the objectives. This knowledge can allow you to give useful advice if you are ever involved in a similar project again.

I was asked to organize a training course that was intended to reduce the number of complaints the company received from customers. My course was an introduction to customer care for junior staff who came into face-to-face contact with the public. I came in on budget and everyone enjoyed the course and said they learned a lot. The supervisors of the people who came on the course were also pleased. However, the number of complaints the company received did not go down. This worried me greatly and I investigated a little further. It turned out that most of the complaints were about delays in processing orders and the inflexible attitude of the office staff who wrote to customers. I realized that there was nothing wrong with my course. It was just that the company had sent the wrong people on it!

Learning from a project

At the end of a project, you have an excellent opportunity to reflect and learn from your successes and failures. Here is a list of questions you should ask yourself.

- Was everyone involved always clear about what they were supposed to do?
- How realistic was the original plan? In what ways did it change?
- How well did I communicate these changes?
- How realistic was the budget?
- How realistic was the schedule?
- What were the strengths and weaknesses of the staff, suppliers and sub-contractors used?
- What planning tools were used and how useful were they?
- What other planning skills do I need to develop?
- What aspects of the project could have gone better?
- How effective were the monitoring and control systems?
- Is there any data about resource use which I can make use of on a future occasion?
- What would I do differently if I were starting the project again?

Activity 26	Ask yourself these questions in relation to a small project in which you have been involved in the past. What lessons can you learn?

However well or badly a project has gone, there are always lessons to be learned for the future. In the long term, these lessons are often much more important and valuable than the outcomes of the individual project itself.

Work study techniques

You also need to evaluate ongoing processes. Because these activities are continuing, and require your constant attention, it is not always easy to step outside and consider if things could be done more effectively.

In this part of the chapter we will describe some of the scientific methods that are used to measure and redesign work processes. Work study originated in the USA. It was developed by F. W. Taylor and F. B. Gilbreth at the turn of the century. It is unlikely that you will be asked to use these techniques yourself in a formal way without receiving specialized training. However, there are some very useful principles involved that should give you some insights into the way your team works.

Method study

This is a technique of looking at how work is organized. It involves these steps:

- selecting the work to be studied
- recording all relevant facts about the present method
- examining these facts critically and in an ordered sequence
- developing the most practical, economic and effective method
- defining the method
- installing the method as standard practice
- maintaining the new method through regular checks.

Method study is a time-consuming process and is usually only used to examine aspects of work that will justify the effort. These could be:

• work which involve a great deal of direct labour
• work for which there is a high demand
• work which causes bottlenecks in the workplace
• work that is very tiring, unpleasant or dangerous.

Investigate 22

Think of two tasks in your own workplace that could be suitable subjects for method study.

The next step is to describe how the work is done at the moment. A diagram known as a **flow process chart** is often used to do this. This chart uses the following five symbols:

◯	Operation – any step in which the material or product is modified or changed
▢	Inspection – checking either the quality or quantity of the product
⇨	Transport – moving from place to place and loading and unloading
◖	Temporary delay – materials waiting for transport, processing or checking that are **not** booked into a recognized store
▽	Storage – materials booked into a recognized store

Figure 3.4

The symbols are drawn on a vertical line. The chart in Figure 3.5 describes part of a manufacturing process.

Other facts about the process, including the time taken to complete each task, may be recorded. Sometimes a plan is drawn to show the physical location at which each part of the operation is performed.

ACTIVITIES MANAGEMENT

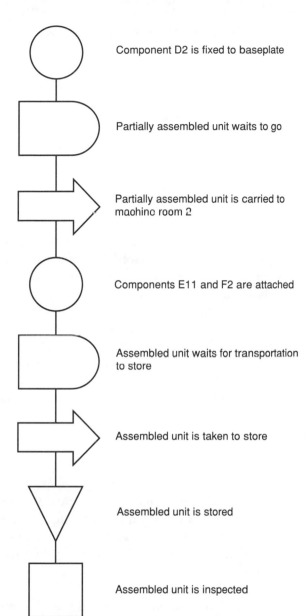

Component D2 is fixed to baseplate

Partially assembled unit waits to go

Partially assembled unit is carried to machine room 2

Components E11 and F2 are attached

Assembled unit waits for transportation to store

Assembled unit is taken to store

Assembled unit is stored

Assembled unit is inspected

Figure 3.5

Activity 27

Draw a flow process chart for a process with which you are familiar.

The next step involves taking a critical look at how the process is performed. A series of questions is asked about every aspect of the process.

How to examine a work process

Purpose	What is done?	Why is it necessary?
Place	Where is it done?	Why here?
Sequence	When is it done relative to other activities?	Why then?
Person	Who does it?	Why this person?
Means	How is it done?	Why by this method?

The aim at this stage is to look for ways in which the process can be improved. It may be possible to eliminate some of the delays, or certain parts of the operation, by doing things in a different order or by using different equipment or work methods.

Ideas for improvements are then discussed with the people who are familiar with the process. The cost, and potential savings, of the new method are calculated. The new method is then worked out in detail and implemented. This may involve new equipment and it may also be necessary to provide training for staff.

Motion economy

Motion economy refers to a series of rules that have been developed to enable human beings to work most effectively. These rules are most useful if you are examining repetitive physical work, but some of the points have a wider relevance.

- Both hands should not be idle at the same time.
- Arm movements should be simultaneous, symmetrical and opposite.
- The minimum movement of the hands and other parts of the body should be required.
- Continuous curved movements are better than jerky movements involving changes of direction.
- Tools and objects being worked on should be placed in fixed positions, so that the worker's movements become automatic.
- Tools and objects being worked on should be placed within easy reach.

- Tools and objects being worked on should be arranged so they can be used in the correct sequence.
- Workers should be comfortably seated at an appropriate height.

| Investigate 23 | Think about how your own desk is organized. Could these rules help you organize it more effectively? |

Ergonomics

Ergonomics is the study of the relationship between people and the environment in which they work. It makes use of information on average body measurements, the way the human body functions and the psychological conditions that people find most motivating.

In ergonomics, the relationship between a person and a machine is studied. This relationship is thought of as a control loop, in which the person receives information from the machine's displays and then uses the machine's controls to activate the machine. You are probably aware of the influence of ergonomics in the design of modern cars. The ease with which the driver can see and interpret the information on the dashboard and operate the clutch, brake, accelerator and steering wheel is an example of ergonomic design. Similar attention can be given to the design of machines used in the workplace.

As well as the design and physical positioning of machine displays and controls, ergonomics also considers heating, lighting, noise and vibration in the workplace. A noisy atmosphere, or one that is too hot or too cold, can be difficult to work in.

The psychological environment is also important. Much has been written about what motivates people to be productive at work. Herzberg developed a theory that people expect certain basic conditions at work, including safe working conditions and good interpersonal relationships. These things, known as **hygiene factors**, would not in themselves motivate people. However, if they were missing, people would be dissatisfied and demotivated. The motivation to work effectively came from another set of factors, which included a sense of achievement, recognition, and responsibility. Motivating

MONITORING ACTIVITIES

factors come from the job itself, not the conditions in which it is performed, but they cannot have an effect unless the hygiene factors are also present.

David McClelland identified three motivating needs that everybody has, each to a greater or lesser extent:

- **the need for affiliation** – people with this need like to work in a group. They enjoy working alongside colleagues whom they know very well. Relationships are very important to them
- **the need for power** – people with this need like to exercise control. They may be good communicators, and also argumentative and demanding. They seek out positions of power
- **the need for achievement** – people who feel this need strongly have a powerful desire for success, and a powerful fear of failure.

According to McClelland, people are motivated to work by their desire to fulfil these needs. You may encourage your team members to work more effectively if you can match individuals to roles in which they are able to fulfil the needs that are most important to them.

Think about the people on your team. Which need is most important to each individual? Have you arranged their roles so that they are able to fulfil these needs?

Adams developed an idea known as the **equity theory**, which states that people are less influenced by the realities of the situation in which they work than by their perception of whether other people are being treated more favourably. If they believe that other workers have better conditions, higher wages or a more reasonable boss, they will become dissatisfied.

Use the three theories outlined here to describe the psychological conditions in which your team works. What could you do to increase their motivation?

Time study

This is a method of measuring the time it takes to perform a task. It is usually applied to repetitive physical jobs. Time study requires a knowledge of statistics and should not be attempted without specialized training. It should only be carried out after a method study has established that an operation is being done in the most effective way.

When a time study is undertaken, an observer notes down all the details of an operation. The operation is then divided up into elements. An element is defined as a task or group of tasks that has a clearly defined end point and which takes not longer than three seconds. The work is then timed repeatedly and an average timing for each element is calculated. From a statistical analysis of these observations, a scale of timings is calculated for people working at slow, steady, brisk, fast and extremely fast levels of performance.

Activity 30

Do you know how quickly your team can complete the tasks you set them? If you are not sure, how could you find out?

Unless your team is engaged in very repetitive work, a time study is probably not appropriate. However, you need to be aware of how long it takes people to do the work you set them. You cannot plan effectively unless you have this knowledge. You can learn a lot by comparing the time that different people take to do the same task.

Summary

When you monitor activities, you should check actual results against your estimates and examine the variance. However, monitoring is not simply a question of progress chasing. You will also need the ability to be flexible and find solutions to unforeseen problems. The key elements that you need to monitor are time, money and quality. It is essential to select indicators that will give you an accurate picture of how activities are proceeding. Do not be tempted to gather too much information. There are several methods of monitoring, including automatic recording, self-monitoring, team meetings and reports. Whatever method or methods you use, make sure that you collect quality information.

MONITORING ACTIVITIES

If you encounter difficulties in the monitoring phase, take a logical approach to problem-solving. Some of your problems may be caused by personality clashes within your team. An understanding of the strengths and weaknesses of your team members can help you. If you have to update your plans, only consider changing your objectives if you have exhausted other possibilities. If you make changes to your instructions, make absolutely sure that everyone involved knows about the new plans. At the end of the planning cycle, it is important to evaluate what happened – and what improvements you could make in the future.

Review and discussion questions

1 What are the characteristics of an effective monitoring system?
2 How would you define quality information for monitoring?
3 What are the four steps in the problem-solving process?
4 What are the advantages and disadvantages of fast tracking?
5 What are the five symbols that are used in a flow process chart and what do they mean?

Case study

Janice, a team leader in an office providing computer support services, has asked three team members to prepare some guidance notes that can be circulated around the organization. The notes are supposed to provide an introduction to databases for staff who have not used them before. The staff who have been delegated to perform this task are:

Rita: a reliable team member who is normally extremely efficient. She is quiet, but she gets on with the job without making a fuss. Janice put her in charge of the group who is writing the notes.

Asif: the youngest and brightest member of the team. He is full of new ideas and the notes were his suggestion in the first place. The rest of the team is slightly suspicious of Asif. He is ambitious and seems destined to go a long way in the organization. He is often impatient with people who do not pick things up as quickly as he does.

John: a stickler for detail. Janice knows that if he is involved in the project, the notes will be 100 per cent accurate. He does not work particularly quickly, but the results are usually worth waiting for.

Janice is expecting to see a first draft of the notes at the end of the month. A week before the deadline, Rita comes to see her. She says: 'It's hopeless! We have got nowhere. Asif keeps coming up with new ideas and saying we ought to start again from scratch. John doesn't know whether he's coming or going.'
What should Janice do?

Work-based assignment

Identify an area of your team's activities with which you are not completely satisfied. What methods do you use to monitor progress? Make some suggestions for ways in which you could improve your system of monitoring.

Action plan

This action plan can be used to improve the performance of your team.

1 Identify a problem area.
2 Define the limits of the problem.
3 Consider the causes of the problem.
4 Talk to the people involved and think of a range of solutions to the problem.
5 Consider the resource implications of the possible solutions.
6 Select the best solution.
7 Brief your team and implement the solution.
8 Monitor what happens.

4 Raw materials, supplies and equipment

Learning objectives

On completion of this chapter you will be able to:

- write a specification for resources
- describe the advantages and disadvantages of different methods of organizing production
- outline the principles of 'just in time' management
- outline the principles of stock control
- take appropriate measures when receiving goods
- explain key issues relating to the care and security of supplies and equipment.

NVQ links

This chapter covers underpinning knowledge required for the vocational qualification in management at level 3 for the mandatory unit:

Unit A1 Maintain activities to meet requirements

A1.1   Maintain work activities to meet requirements
A1.2   Maintain healthy, safe and productive working conditions
A1.3   Make recommendations for improvements to work activities

Introduction

All organizations require some physical resources in order to carry out their work. These resources can take many forms, including:

- stock for sale to retail customers
- raw materials

- components
- office supplies
- machinery
- other equipment.

Some of these things, such as machinery, may last for many years while others, such as raw materials, are consumed on a daily basis. If an organization does not have the resources it needs, its processes will grind to a halt. An organization must therefore make sure that it has a guaranteed supply of resources. You may remember from Chapter 1 that an organization's suppliers are as important to it as its customers.

However, there is another aspect to the issue of supplies. Most organizations have a large amount of money tied up in physical resources. This cash is not bringing in any income until it is used – and its cost can be passed on to the customer. For example, a shoe shop will have thousands of pounds of stock on its shelves and in its stockroom. This stock does not produce income until customers pay for individual pairs of shoes. A design group may have invested thousands of pounds in new computer equipment to produce the latest graphic animations. These computers do not earn anything until clients pay for the work that they were used to produce.

All organizations have to perform a balancing act with their physical resources. They cannot afford to run out of supplies or equipment – but neither can they afford to invest too much capital in these things. In this chapter we will look at some of the ways in which organizations manage this equation.

Purchasing and supply systems

Purchasing is the way in which supplies are obtained from outside an organization. In many large organizations, only relatively trivial purchases are made by individual departments. In a business of any size, purchasing is frequently done by a dedicated department. There are several advantages to centralizing the purchasing function:

- buying in bulk can result in economies of scale
- suppliers are likely to value important customers and provide other benefits, such as fast delivery

RAW MATERIALS, SUPPLIES AND EQUIPMENT

- specifications can be set centrally and produce greater consistency throughout the organization
- it is possible to invest time in researching the best suppliers
- administrative costs are lower because fewer invoices have to be processed
- the payment process can be streamlined
- a greater level of control over expenditure can be achieved.

However, central purchasing also has a few disadvantages. Here are some examples:

> *All the computers in the building are bought centrally. The trouble is, the purchasing department doesn't really understand what we need in the design office. IT equipment is moving so fast these days, you have to be working in the field to know what are the features to go for. In purchasing, they haven't got our expertise.*

> *When I go into our local stationers shop, I can have a look around and the manager will tell me if he has got any interesting new lines. That is the way I came across some fluorescent markers that we are using all the time now. If I get my stationery from central purchasing, the range is much narrower and I don't get the personal service.*

> *I needed some shelving for a new office. I looked in the catalogue of the supplier that central purchasing uses. All the shelving was expensive and not particularly suitable. Since it was my budget I was spending, I bought some cheap and very attractive shelves from a local pine shop.*

Central purchasing may not have the expert knowledge required for some specialist purchases. Some managers also feel that they gain more from having a personal relationship with their suppliers. What is more, budget holders sometimes like to retain control of the way they spend their money and believe that they can negotiate better deals than a centralized purchasing department.

What supplies are bought centrally in your organization? What supplies are purchased by your own unit or section? What are the advantages and disadvantages of each system?

Selecting and obtaining resources

The process of selecting and obtaining new resources is made up of several steps:

1 identifying the need
2 specifying exactly what you need
3 identifying possible suppliers
4 selecting the best supplier
5 negotiating with the supplier
6 receiving and checking the resources
7 monitoring the resources in use.

It is very important to remember that the process should begin when you realize you have a need for a resource. Too often, people are tempted to buy new products just because they are available. You are probably aware of expensive equipment that has been purchased by your organization that has never been fully utilized.

The specification stage is crucial. You may specify the characteristics that you want the resources to have. These could include:

- conforms to a particular standard
- is able to perform certain tasks
- works to a given tolerance
- can be used at a given temperature range
- measures a particular size.

You should also think about other aspects of the purchase, including:

- price
- reputation of manufacturer
- durability
- upgradability
- ease of use.

Sometimes you cannot have all the features you would like. In this case, it is useful to make up a list of 'musts' and 'wants'. This will help you decide which option is most suitable to your needs.

You have to communicate your specification to the individual or department who will actually be making the purchase. This may be done in writing, or by providing a sample or even a drawing, if appropriate.

Activity 32

Write a specification for a piece of equipment you need in your department.

Once you have prepared your specification, the purchasing process may be controlled by the purchasing department. If it is not, you will have to select a supplier yourself. Four issues are important here:

- price
- quality
- delivery
- service.

It is important to shop around. Different suppliers can offer exactly the same items at very different prices. They can also offer similar models at varying prices. In this context, quality refers to the degree to which the item conforms to the specifications you have set. Delivery means the time you will have to wait to receive the item, and the degree to which you can rely on it arriving when promised. You may also have to consider the quantity that will be delivered at one time. Here are two comments from a restaurant owner:

> *I found a very cheap supplier of new potatoes. However, the price he quoted only applied if I was prepared to buy ten bags at once. That was far too much for my needs, so I had to go elsewhere.*

> *I also found a local farm that was making speciality cheeses. I would have loved to have served them in my restaurant, but the farm was working on a very small scale and was only able to accept an order for one cheese every two weeks. If I had done that, it would have meant disappointing customers, so I decided against it.*

Service refers to the extra help you can expect from the supplier, both before and after you make the purchase. If you are buying something that is crucial to your operation, is likely to need adjustment, will need replacement parts or is difficult to use, this is an important issue.

| **Activity 33** | Think about the purchase you specified in the last activity. How important are price, quality, delivery and service when the choice of supplier is made? |

Many organizations draw up lists of approved suppliers. They investigate these businesses in detail and may, in addition to the issues discussed already, take ethical or environmental considerations into account.

The final stages of the purchasing process will be dealt with later in this chapter.

Methods of organizing production

The way in which production is organized has implications for when supplies are needed. Traditionally, there are three methods that are used:

- project (or jobbing shop) production
- batch production
- continuous process.

Project production

This involves delivering a series of 'one-off' products or services, each of which is tailored to the specific needs of the customer. You may have experienced this type of process if you have had a meal at a top-class restaurant or perhaps been involved in the commissioning of a video or an advertising campaign. Projects are expensive and they are only used where quality is extremely important to the customer. If you were buying a tailor-made suit, you would expect to pay more than you would for an off-the-peg item. You might also be prepared to wait a little time for your suit to be made, or to pay even more to have the work done immediately.

This method is used in situations where there is a small volume of work and a great variety of products. Supplies are purchased in small quantities as and when they are needed. The higher costs that this involves are relatively unimportant, because they can be passed on to the customer, who is prepared to pay more for a product that exactly meets his or her requirements.

Batch production

As the name suggests, batch production involves working on products or services in batches. Here are some examples of batch production:

- a printer runs off 1000 copies of a poster
- a restaurant makes up a large quantity of a sauce at the beginning of the day
- an office collects all the expense claims together and processes them together once a month
- an office cleaner empties all the waste paper bins on one floor.

Batch production is more cost-effective and therefore less expensive than project work, but it does have certain disadvantages. If you go into a baker's shop and discover they have run out of bread, you cannot expect them to make a loaf especially for you. You will have to wait until the next batch is prepared. Where industrial processes are involved, this can mean a substantial delay. The first products in a batch to undergo a process may have to wait for the rest of the batch to be finished, so they can go on to the next stage together. The products or services prepared in this way will all be very similar and the customer cannot expect the same level of control over the end-product.

Batch production allows an organization to make a variety of different products using the same basic equipment. However, before a batch of products is manufactured, the equipment has to be set up and prepared. During this set-up time, nothing is being produced.

An organization that uses this method will need a variety of different supplies, but many of these will be required on an intermittent basis. Supplies must be available when a batch is ready to go through. If there are long gaps between batches of a particular product, the organization may face storage problems.

Continuous process

The third method of production is continuous. The same equipment is used to make the same products all the time. This method is also known as assembly belt production. The advantage is that costs are kept to a minimum. Because demand can be predicted and supplies are being used up continuously, they can be purchased in bulk quantities. Set-up time is also greatly reduced, which produces another saving. However, the continuous process method is very inflexible. It results in a uniform product and it can be difficult to vary the rate of production.

Activity 34

Which of these methods is suitable for:

1 a large volume of similar products
2 a medium volume of similar products
3 a small volume of dissimilar products.

See Feedback section for answer to this activity.

Just in time

Just in time (JIT) production is an alternative to the three methods we have described. It originated in Japan and brings together some of the best features of the project, batch and continuous process methods. Many of the features of JIT were developed by a production engineer, Taiichi Ohno, who is known as the 'Father of Just in Time'.

JIT came about after the Second World War, when Japan was rebuilding its economy. Land prices were high and factory space was expensive, so the maximum use had to be made of it. Japanese managers realized that most of the space in their factories was being used to store raw materials, work-in-progress and finished work that was waiting to be sold.

These three issues were tackled in different ways. The need to store large quantities of raw materials was avoided by buying from suppliers who were able to deliver small quantities as they were required. The amount of work-in-progress was minimized by reducing the size of batches. Instead of having a bin by the side of a machine, where finished parts would be placed before moving on to the next process, parts were passed directly from process to process, reducing waiting times dramatically. This was made possible by redesigning the layout of the factory floor. Instead of having separate areas of the factory dedicated to different processes, machines were brought together and placed side by side, in a U-shape.

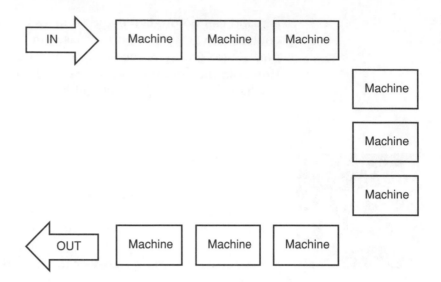

Figure 4.1

All these machines could be operated by one or two people. These workers could work continuously because they did not have to wait for batches of components to be delivered from another area of the factory.

It is not always possible to place machines in close proximity to each other. In these situations, JIT makes use of a system known as **kabans**. (Kaban is the Japanese word for ticket.) The idea behind kabans is that products are only made when they are required. When an order is received in a JIT factory, a ticket is issued authorizing the manufacture of the product. The supervisor receives the ticket and starts gathering together the components that will be needed. He or she issues separate kabans to the workers who will make the components.

A JIT factory is very flexible. It can respond to the needs of individual customers and workers can switch from one product to another slightly different one very quickly. Materials and half-completed work are not left waiting around to be used. It is not necessary to store large quantities of finished products, because products are manufactured quickly, when they are needed.

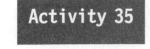

Think about the way work is organized in your own organization. Could any of the ideas associated with JIT be used?

ACTIVITIES MANAGEMENT

JIT was developed in conjunction with the approach to quality that was discussed in Chapter 1. One of the key ideas that lies behind both systems is that the needs of customers, whether they are internal or external, should drive the production process.

Stock control

Despite the advantages of JIT, most organizations still have to keep large amounts of stock. In this section we will examine the issues that need to be considered in relation to the storage and organization of stock. In essence, these principles are exactly the same as those that people use (or should use) to organize their kitchen cupboards.

At one time or another, you have probably had one of these experiences:

A you are cooking a special meal and find that one of the ingredients you need is missing from your cupboard

B a week later, you find a packet of the missing ingredient hidden behind a tin of beans

C you buy a jar of coffee, only to discover that someone else has bought one the previous day and put it in the cupboard

D you discover that another member of the family has raided the cupboard and taken something that you need to cook a meal

E you find an unlabelled container in the cupboard and are not sure whether it is full of cornflour or icing sugar, so decide to throw it away

F you clear out your cupboards and find three packets of an expensive ingredient, two of which are past their sell-by date

G you discover a pot of jam with mould growing on it at the back of the kitchen cupboard.

These events happen because of inadequate stock control. In the kitchen, experiences like these are annoying. In a business, they can be commercially disastrous. The principles of stock control that are illustrated here are:

1 stock must be kept in conditions where it will not deteriorate

2 it must be possible to locate individual items of stock easily and quickly

3 access to stock must be restricted to authorized persons
4 records of movements into and out of stock must be kept
5 all stock must be clearly identified
6 stock that has a limited life must be used in rotation
7 an up-to-date record of stock should be available.

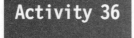

Can you match the problems in the kitchen cupboard to the principles?

See Feedback section for answer to this activity.

The security of stock and the conditions in which it is kept will be discussed later in the chapter. The other principles are all related to record keeping.

In the past, stock control was usually done on a series of cards. Each type of stock had a separate card, containing the following information:

• name, description and code number of item
• date of stock movement
• reference number
• number of items received or removed from stock or allocated to a particular purpose
• number of items remaining in stock after each stock movement.

After each movement of stock, the balance would be 'proved', or checked, by performing a small calculation. Details of stock movements would also be kept in chronological order in a journal.

Computerization has made the process of stock control much less labour intensive. Programs are now available that can immediately tell the stock keeper:

• how many of each stock item are currently in stock
• when items were removed or added to stock
• where the items are stored
• whether there is enough stock for a specific purpose
• the details of the supplier (and alternative suppliers) for each item of stock
• maximum and minimum stock levels.

Some programs will even take an order from the factory, work out a Bill of Materials (a list of the materials or components required) and then prepare the orders to go out to suppliers if any items cannot be supplied directly from stock.

Find out what stock is kept within your organization. What system is used to record stock movements?

Procedures for receiving goods

When goods are supplied by one organization to another, the purchaser has some legal protection. The Sale of Goods Act 1979 states that certain terms are to be implied in contracts for the sale of goods, regardless of whether these terms are actually stated. Goods must be:

- as described
- of satisfactory quality
- fit for any purpose which the consumer makes known to the seller for which he wishes to use the goods.

Goods are considered to be of satisfactory quality if they reach the standard which a reasonable person would regard as satisfactory, taking into account the price and any description. Purchasers must have an opportunity to examine goods before they accept them. It is important to remember that, under the Act, it is the seller rather than the manufacturer who is responsible, so if you believe you have been sold sub-standard goods, you should complain to your supplier, not the company that originally made the goods.

If the buyers discover that the goods are not of satisfactory quality, they are entitled, if they act within a reasonable time, to reject the goods and demand a refund. The phrase 'a reasonable time' is not defined and is open to interpretation and argument. However, even if a reasonable time has elapsed before buyers discover that the goods are faulty, they may still be entitled to have the goods repaired or replaced, and receive compensation for any damage done because the goods were faulty, although they cannot ask for a refund of the purchase price.

The Sale of Goods Act 1979 does not apply in quite the same way to businesses as it does to ordinary consumers. For

RAW MATERIALS, SUPPLIES AND EQUIPMENT

example, if a second-hand dealer sells a van to an individual and the van proves to have faults that were not pointed out to the purchaser, he or she may be able to claim that the goods were not of satisfactory quality. However, if the dealer sells the same van to another dealer, it may be assumed that both parties have the same level of expert knowledge and the purchaser should have discovered the faults.

Another important piece of legislation is the Unfair Contract Terms Act 1977. This also has different implications for business customers and ordinary consumers. Individuals are protected against unfair terms that a seller puts into a contract. However, the Act states that when goods are sold or hired to non-consumers (that is, other businesses), the implied conditions of the Sale of Goods Act 1979 can be excluded, but only in so far as the exclusion satisfies the test of reasonableness. This means that commercial organizations are free to agree contracts between themselves on terms that they both agree.

So what does all this mean in practice? Organizations have to be more careful than ordinary consumers that they do not accept sub-standard goods. There may be terms in the contract that exclude the purchaser from some of the protection provided by consumer legislation. Instead of simply returning faulty goods and demanding a refund, a business may have to take a supplier to court for breach of contract. This would be time-consuming and expensive.

There are normally two stages to receiving goods. When the delivery arrives, a representative of the receiving organization must sign a receipt. This signature does not necessarily mean that the goods have been accepted. In most situations, it is completely impractical to unpack a delivery and examine the contents while the driver waits for your verdict. At this stage, it is only necessary to check that the number of packages tallies with any accompanying documentation and that the packaging does not appear to be damaged.

You should, however, check the goods as soon as reasonably possible. When you do so, you should look out for any notices or warnings that tell you that, in performing a certain action, you are accepting the terms and conditions of sale. For example, if you start using a piece of equipment and then discover that it is not exactly what you ordered, you may find it difficult to persuade the supplier to take it back. If you are in any doubt, get advice from your manager. It is better to delay using a piece of equipment than to find yourself in a situation where your organization has to go to court to obtain redress.

Many organizations have agreed procedures with particular suppliers. Here is an example from an office that purchases computers for a large hospital:

When a computer arrives, we are supposed to unpack it within a certain number of days and test it on the workbench. If it doesn't work, it is classified as 'dead on arrival' and we send it back immediately. If we leave it longer, or something happens after we deliver the machine to the office where it will be used, anything that goes wrong is classified as a 'fault'. We then call in the suppliers' service engineers. They either repair the machine or replace it.

Investigate 25

Obtain a copy of the terms and conditions used by one of your organization's suppliers. What opportunity do they give the purchaser to examine the goods? At what point is the purchaser deemed to have accepted the goods?

Security and care of supplies and equipment

In this section we will consider how you look after the supplies and equipment that have been purchased. Some of the issues discussed here are relevant to goods that are stored centrally. Others also apply to the goods that are being stored or are actually in use in individual departments.

Where materials are stored

If large quantities of supplies must be stored, the store is normally situated in an area where delivery vehicles can have access. This is usually well away from the entrances used by customers or members of staff. A separate entrance for deliveries makes it easier to ensure security. There are also safety and aesthetic reasons for keeping delivery traffic away from areas to which members of the public have access.

If the site is very large, or some supplies are needed on a regular basis by particular departments, there may also be smaller storage areas in other parts of the premises.

RAW MATERIALS, SUPPLIES AND EQUIPMENT

Activity 37

What do you think are the advantages and disadvantages of having several smaller storage areas?

See Feedback section for answer to this activity.

Security

There are several ways of maintaining the security of storage areas, including:

- restricting access to authorized personnel only
- alarms, locks and other security devices
- rigorous stock control.

Earlier in the chapter, some of the records relating to stock were described. It is relatively easy to have an up-to-date record of every item of stock. However, just because an item is listed on a computer or a record card, does not necessarily mean that the item is still present in the stockroom. In order to verify this, it is necessary to make a physical check of the stock. This involves going round the shelves and actually counting what is there.

There are several reasons why the stock on the shelves may not match the stock listed in the records. Stock may have been stolen or placed in the wrong position on the shelves. Stock may have been damaged while it was in store. Too many (or too few) items may have been issued in response to an order. The records of what has been received, issued or returned to the stockroom may be inaccurate or out-of-date. Information technology can make the process of checking much simpler than it used to be. Computer programs can automatically generate an up-to-date stock list, arranged in the same order as the items should be arranged on the shelves.

Security remains an important issue for equipment and supplies when they are actually in use. Large and expensive items can be security-coded, but smaller items can be removed by intruders, members of the public, or by staff. Some people think that it is acceptable to take small, inexpensive items from their workplace, and would be surprised to hear this practice described as theft.

ACTIVITIES MANAGEMENT

Ask your colleagues whether they think that an employee should be disciplined for any of the following actions:

- taking a pencil home from work
- using office stationery for their own purposes
- in a supermarket, eating a piece of fruit that was past its sell-by date and was going to be thrown away
- taking a computer disk
- taking a toilet roll.

The way your colleagues respond to these questions may be related to the policy that operates in your organization. Some workplaces are quite relaxed about the disappearance of small items. Others take a very strong line indeed and would consider dismissing an employee for any of the offences described here.

Locating items of stock

Stock must be organized so that it is easy to locate items when they are needed. One way to do this is to have a structure of labelled bays and shelves and keep a record of where everything is kept. In a smaller store, or in a situation where the items of stock are instantly recognizable, it may be sufficient always to keep the same things in the same places.

Stock that will deteriorate over time should be used on a first in, first out basis. Some stockrooms physically move the stock, so that the older items are placed at the front. Another system is to have two adjacent storage areas for items that will deteriorate. Old stock is placed in one place, and new stock in the other. The new stock is not touched until the old supply is exhausted.

Another principle to bear in mind when organizing stores is that the items that are required most frequently should be the most accessible.

Examine the supplies that are kept in your department or section. Is it possible for anyone, apart from the person who is responsible for the stores, to locate particular items? What arrangements are made to ensure that old stock gets used first? Are the most frequently requested items the most accessible?

RAW MATERIALS, SUPPLIES AND EQUIPMENT

Conditions of storage

Some supplies will deteriorate and become unusable if they are kept in unsuitable conditions. Here are some examples:

- food that has been cook-chilled can be stored for up to five days, as long as it is kept at a temperature of between 0°C and 3°C
- paper for a photocopier or printer that is kept in a damp atmosphere will curl and jam the machine
- computer disks can become unreadable if they are exposed to electromagnetism
- some electronic equipment can be damaged if it is exposed to dust or smoke
- anything made of ferrous-based metal (from paperclips to frying pans) can become rusty if it is kept in damp conditions
- toner will be unusable if it is exposed to light
- water-based paints will separate if they are allowed to freeze
- videotapes are susceptible to mildew if they are kept in damp conditions.

Most ordinary office supplies will have a long shelf-life if they are kept in normal office conditions. However, storage areas are not always maintained to the same temperature and humidity as the areas in which people work.

By law, the temperature at which foodstuffs are stored must be very carefully regulated. Other supplies, including some of the raw materials used in industrial processes, often require specialized storage conditions, too.

Investigate 28

Examine the stores that are kept in your department or section. What is their anticipated shelf-life? What conditions should they be kept in? Are they kept in these conditions?

Summary

Organizations have a great deal of money tied up in their supplies and must take this aspect of operations seriously. The purchasing of supplies may be done centrally, or devolved to individual departments or sections. The process of purchasing supplies should begin by defining the requirements and preparing a specification.

ACTIVITIES MANAGEMENT

Different ways of organizing production, such as project, batch and continuous process, have varying implications for supplies. Just in time, a system invented in Japan as part of their development of quality management, reduces the amount of supplies, work-in-hand and finished goods to the minimum.

The management of supplies and other stock involves considering access, record-keeping, rotation of stock and security. The conditions in which stock is kept can also be very important.

Under UK law, businesses have slightly different rights to ordinary consumers. It is essential to consult the terms and conditions that are agreed with individual suppliers.

Review and discussion questions

1 What are the advantages of centralizing the purchasing function?
2 What four issues should you bear in mind when choosing a supplier?
3 What is a kaban?
4 If the goods you buy are faulty, who should you complain to?
5 Can you suggest six reasons why the stock on the shelves does not correspond to the stock in the records?

Case study When Cara took over the General Office, one of her responsibilities was to look after the supply of stationery to the building. The company employed fifty-five people. All stationery was ordered from one supplier. Exactly the same order had been submitted each month for the past year.

When Cara opened the door of the stationery store, she was shocked. The door was not locked and staff from all over the building simply came and helped themselves to stationery as and when they needed it. The room was a mess. Old and new stock was mixed up. Some reams of paper were stored on their side and had become bent. At the back of one of the shelves she found some sheets of cardboard that showed signs of mildew. She also found some mouse droppings on the floor.

What should Cara do?

RAW MATERIALS, SUPPLIES AND EQUIPMENT

Work-based assignment

Write a short report on your organization's procedures for purchasing and receiving supplies.

Action plan

This action plan can be used when you are purchasing supplies.

1 Prepare a specification for the item you want to buy.
2 Identify possible suppliers.
3 Compare the quality, price, delivery and service offered by these suppliers.
4 Select the most appropriate supplier.
5 Check terms and condition of sale.
6 Make the purchase.
7 Receive the item.
8 Check that the supplies are satisfactory.

5 Health and safety

Learning objectives

On completion of this chapter you will be able to:

- describe the roles of Government organizations responsible for health and safety
- outline the contents of the Health and Safety at Work Act 1974
- identify other important health and safety legislation
- describe the responsibilities for health and safety of employers and employees
- describe the contents of a typical health and safety policy
- conduct a risk assessment
- list the main points to remember when dealing with emergencies
- describe the procedure to use when reporting an accident.

NVQ links

This chapter covers much of the underpinning knowledge required for the vocational qualification in management at level 3 for the mandatory unit:

Unit A1 Maintain activities to meet requirements

A1.2   Maintain healthy, safe and productive working conditions
A1.3   Make recommendations for improvements to work activities

Introduction

It is possible that you turned to this chapter in the book without a great deal of enthusiasm. Health and safety is often thought of as a necessary, but not particularly exciting, topic. The rules and regulations associated with it can be difficult to understand and are frequently time-consuming to put into practice. If, however, you have had direct experience of someone being injured or made ill in the workplace, you will have no doubts about the importance of this chapter.

Here are some personal stories.

I was operating a fixed saw in a carpentry workshop. There was one man who was always messing around, annoying people. One afternoon he started on one of the others who was standing right behind me. I turned round quickly and the blade of the saw went right through my finger, slicing it down behind the nail.

I had to give up nursing, which was a job I loved, because of chronic back pain which developed through lifting patients.

The maintenance staff decided to remove the door of one of the lock-up sheds. They shouldn't have touched the door, since they didn't know what they were doing, and it was on very heavy-duty springs. Anyway, the door suddenly bounced upwards, catching one of the men on the side of the head. He was catapulted across the yard and didn't regain consciousness for 24 hours.

We were very short of space in the office and there was no room on my desk to put the papers I was transcribing. I had to sit typing at a strange angle for hours on end. My wrists started to give me a lot of pain and I was diagnosed with RSI. I had to give up my job. The company gave me several thousand pounds compensation, but I am still in pain and will not be able to do a job that involves typing again.

You may know of similar stories yourself. People's health may be damaged at work because the working conditions are inherently dangerous. In other situations, rules that are intended to protect people are ignored or broken.

About 23 million working days are lost through work-related injuries every year. For employers, this represents a very significant financial loss. For the individuals involved, accidents in the workplace and unhealthy working practices can change their lives.

As a team leader, you are in a good position to influence health and safety within your place of work. You are close enough to the operational level to know what risks people are taking in their day-to-day work. You also have the opportunity (and the duty) to inform and influence higher levels of management about health and safety issues that they need to take more seriously.

Health and safety and the law

Organizations promoting health and safety

There are two main Government organizations with responsibility for health and safety in the UK.

The Health and Safety Commission

The Health and Safety Commission (HSC) has responsibility for developing policy on health and safety at work, including guidance, codes of practice, and proposals for regulations. It is accountable to parliament through the Secretary of State for Education and Employment. The HSC has an obligation to consult those who would be affected by new regulations and make recommendations to the Secretary of State. The HSC has seven advisory committees dealing with specific topics such as toxic substances, genetic manipulation and safety of nuclear installations, and some specific industry advisory committees.

The Health and Safety Executive

The Health and Safety Executive (HSE) is the primary instrument for carrying out the policies of the HSC. It has day-to-day responsibility for enforcing health and safety law, except where local authorities are responsible. In offices, shops, warehouses, restaurants and hotels, health and safety legislation is enforced by local authority inspectors, working under guidance from the HSE. The HSE publishes a wide range of leaflets and information sheets on health and safety matters. A large number of these publications can now be viewed on the Internet.

The HSE's website includes information on specific types of risk, such as manual handling, working in confined spaces and slips, trips and falls. It also provides the full text of leaflets relevant to a series of different workplaces, including agriculture, mines and quarries, motor industry, offices, textiles and woodworking.

HEALTH AND SAFETY

Investigate 29

If you have access to the Internet, visit the HSE's website. The address is:

http://www.open.gov.uk/hse/hsehome.htm

What information can you find that is relevant to your place of work?

Other health and safety organizations

In addition to the HSC and HSE, several other organizations are interested in safety in the workplace. Many professional bodies (such as, for example, the British Constructional Steelwork Association, the Royal College of Nursing, the Hospitality Training Foundation and the Institution of Electrical Engineers) advise their members on health and safety. Other organizations have been set up specifically to promote safe working practices. An example is the Suzy Lamplugh Trust, a charity that aims to help people who work alone to lead safer lives. It was established by Diana Lamplugh after the disappearance of her daughter, who worked as an estate agent and was last seen leaving a property with a client.

The Health and Safety at Work Act 1974

This Act, known as HASAWA, is the most important piece of health and safety legislation. It imposes responsibilities on employers to ensure their staff work in an environment that minimizes risk to their health and safety and also outlines the duties required of managers and individual staff members. We will look in detail at these responsibilities later in the chapter.

There are several other regulations, dealing with particular hazards and types of work, attached to the HASAWA. They include the Electricity at Work Regulations 1989, the Noise at Work Regulations 1989 and the Reporting of Injuries, Diseases and Dangerous Occurrences Regulations 1985 (RIDDOR).

The Control of Substances Hazardous to Health Regulations 1988 (COSHH) also comes under the HASAWA. It covers any use of dangerous chemicals, cleaning materials or other substances that are toxic, irritant or harmful in some way. Control measures that an employer might take to prevent an employee from being exposed to hazardous substances could include:

- changing the process so that the hazardous substance is no longer used, or substituting the hazardous substance with a safer one, or alternatively:
- employing safe procedures for working and handling (for example, providing protective clothing and following manufacturers' guidelines)
- ensuring adequate ventilation
- totally enclosing the process, or partially enclosing the process and using extraction equipment.

Other health and safety legislation

Other pieces of legislation relating to health in safety in specific types of workplace include:

- The Offices, Shops and Railway Premises Act 1963
- The Factories Act 1961
- Fire Precautions Act 1971
- Mines and Quarries Act 1954
- Nuclear Installations Act 1965
- Agriculture (Safety, Health and Welfare Provisions) Act 1956.

Other sets of regulations (as opposed to Acts), include:

- The Management of Health and Safety at Work Regulations 1992
- Health and Safety (Consultation with Employees) Regulations 1996
- Safety Representatives and Safety Committees Regulations 1977
- Workplace (Health, Safety and Welfare) Regulations 1992
- Control of Lead at Work Regulations 1980 (updated 1988)
- Chemical (Hazard Information and Packaging for Supply) Regulations 1994
- The Control of Asbestos at Work Regulations 1987
- The Asbestos (Licensing) Regulations 1983
- The Asbestos (Prohibitions) Regulations 1992
- The Health and Safety (First Aid) Regulations 1981
- The Construction Regulations 1961 (includes General Provisions, Lifting Operations, Working Places 1966 and Design and Maintenance 1994)

- The Health and Safety Information for Employees Regulations 1989 (modified 1995)
- Manual Handling Operations Regulations 1992
- Noise at Work Regulations 1989
- Electricity at Work Regulations 1989
- Provision and Use of Work Equipment Regulations 1992
- Power Presses Regulations 1965 and 1972
- Pressure Systems and Transportable Gas Containers Regulations 1989
- Construction (Health, Safety and Welfare) Regulations 1994
- Construction (Design and Management) Regulations 1996
- Confined Spaces Regulations 1997
- Highly Flammable Liquids and Liquefied Petroleum Gases Regulations 1972
- Ionising Radiations Regulations 1985.

Six sets of EU health and safety regulations came into force in 1993, dealing with:

- the management of health and safety
- the provision and use of work equipment
- personal protective equipment
- manual handling equipment
- display screen equipment
- general health, safety and welfare in the workplace.

You do not have to be familiar with all these Acts and regulations, but you need to be aware of the main points of those Acts and regulations that are relevant to your work.

Investigate 30

Look through the list of legislation and regulations given above. Make a note of any that you think are relevant to your place of work. Talk to a safety representative within your organization. What information can he or she give you about these Acts and regulations?

Responsibility for health and safety

The Health and Safety at Work Act 1974 lists the duties of employers and employees.

The responsibilities of employers

Employers have a duty to:

- make the workplace safe and without risks to health
- keep dust, fumes and noise under control
- ensure that plant and machinery are safe and that safe systems of work are set and followed
- ensure that articles and substances are moved, stored and used safely
- provide adequate welfare facilities
- provide employees with the information, instruction, training and supervision necessary for their health and safety.

Employers must also:

- draw up a health and safety policy statement (if there are five or more employees) which describes the health and safety organization and arrangements that are in force
- bring the health and safety policy statement to the attention of employees
- provide free of charge any protective clothing or equipment that is specifically required by health and safety law
- report certain injuries, diseases and dangerous occurrences to the enforcing authority
- provide adequate first aid facilities
- consult a safety representative, if one is appointed by a recognized trade union, about matters affecting the health and safety of employees
- set up a safety committee, if asked in writing to do so by two or more safety representatives
- employers must also take precautions against fire, provide adequate means of escape and means for fighting fire.

In many workplaces, there may be specific dangers and employers may also have other duties. Here are some examples:

- take adequate precautions against explosions of flammable dust or gas
- ensure that employees do not have to lift, carry or move any load so heavy that it is likely to injure them
- guard securely all dangerous parts of machines

- provide employees with suitable eye protection or protective equipment for certain jobs
- take precautions against danger from electrical equipment and radiation
- ensure that employees, especially young people, are properly trained or under adequate supervision before using dangerous machines
- ensure that floors, steps, stairs, ladders, passages and gangways are well constructed and maintained and not obstructed.

Investigate 31

Which of the employer's duties listed above are relevant to your place of work? Are you aware of any accidents or damage to health that has happened because your employer did **not** do these things?

The responsibilities of employees

Of course, all the safety rules and regulations in the world are useless if they are ignored by the people to whom they apply. Employers need the co-operation of the workforce if they are to protect their health and safety. The HASAWA sets out the following duties for employees:

- taking reasonable care for their own health and safety and that of others who may be affected by what they do or do not do
- co-operating with the employer on health and safety
- not interfering with or misusing anything provided for their health, safety or welfare
- using equipment provided by the employer in accordance with training and instruction provided by the employer (in compliance with the requirements imposed on the employer by, or under, relevant statutory provision).

Employees should inform the employer (or someone with a health and safety responsibility) of any work situation that would represent a serious and immediate danger to health and safety, and of any matter that they reasonably consider to represent a shortcoming in the employer's provision for health and safety.

Your responsibilities as team leader

As a team leader, you share the same health and safety duties as other employees. You must take reasonable care in your own actions, co-operate with your employers and use any equipment provided for your health and safety in a proper manner. In addition, you have a responsibility for the health and safety of the members of your team, and anyone who may be affected by anything they do (or do not do). If an accident results from a failure on your part, your organization could be prosecuted. The HASAWA makes it clear that ultimate responsibility for health and safety lies with the highest levels of management. However, this responsibility can be delegated to others within the organization, including yourself.

You must ensure that members of your team follow health and safety rules at all times. Some of these precautions may slow up people's work and they may be tempted to ignore them. You may even be tempted to turn a blind eye yourself on some occasions. It is also possible that your managers will expect you to cut corners. You must resist the temptation to break the rules, whoever tries to influence you to do so. Accidents are much more likely to happen when people are working under pressure. If someone is injured, you will find it difficult to justify any lapses of vigilance.

You must also look out for risks that are not covered by the existing rules. These may be new hazards, arising from new equipment or new processes – or simply hazards that nobody has thought of before. Later in the chapter, we will discuss how to assess these risks.

Penalties

If an organization fails to provide and maintain a safe and healthy working environment, legal action can be taken. This can result in a fine, or even, in some circumstances, closure of the premises. Persistent offenders could face imprisonment. Employees who do not carry out their duties with respect to health and safety could face disciplinary action by their employers. In some cases, this can lead to dismissal. In extreme situations, individuals can be also be prosecuted.

The following cases are adapted from press releases issued by the HSE.

CASE 1

In November 1995 a multi-national chemical company occupying a manufacturing site based in the East Midlands engaged a small local contractor to dismantle a redundant road tanker loading gantry. There was inadequate liaison with the contractor which lead to the adoption of an unsafe system of work. The outcome was the premature uncontrolled collapse of the structure together with the overturning of the works crane. Nobody was seriously injured and there was no chemical release, even though the crane jib landed on the main acid export pipeline. This buckled but did not fracture. Both parties were prosecuted in the Crown Court in December 1996. The judge placed most of the blame on the chemical company, and this was reflected in the respective penalties. The chemical company was fined £10 000 with £6000 costs. The contractor was fined £1000 with £339 costs.

CASE 2

In May 1994 two contractor's employees were found unconscious inside the reactor vessel of a small North West chemical manufacturing company. The workmen had been using an adhesive containing a flammable and volatile solvent to fit a rubber lining to the inside of the reactor and had been overcome by the fumes. Employees of the chemical company who tried to rescue the contractors were also affected by the fumes. Employees of both the contractor and the chemical manufacturing company required hospital treatment as a result of the incident. No initial site assessment was completed to identify the precautions and arrangements needed to secure a safe system of work for the job. The contractors did not use breathing apparatus or safety harnesses and no one stayed outside the confined space of the reactor vessel to keep watch on them. No permit to work had been issued to specify the safety arrangements for the completion of the work and the means of access into the reactor vessel were unsatisfactory. The chemical company did not have emergency procedures and an absence of any training or practice to complete an emergency rescue from a confined space lead to their own employees getting injured as well. Both the contractor and partners of the chemical company were prosecuted and each party was fined £20 000. The penalty against the contractor was subsequently reduced to £15 000 on appeal.

CASE 3

On 10 August 1992 contractors carrying out spot welding on the steel doors of an explosives magazine accidentally ignited the fireworks contained within. Approximately 17 tonnes of fireworks were consumed in the fire. Fortunately nobody was injured but, in addition to destruction of the stock, the magazine suffered considerable damage. The company, a small business relatively new to the industry, had inadequate procedures for the control of contractors and did not operate a permit to work system. At the time of the accident the contractors held no permit containing advice on precautions. The company was prosecuted and was fined £1000. The insurance company refused to pay compensation because of the company's negligence and it almost put the owner out of business.

CASE 4

Texaco Ltd and Gulf Oil (Great Britain) Ltd were each fined £100 000, following the incident at Pembroke Cracking Company's facility at the Milford Haven refinery site on 24 July 1994. Texaco and Gulf, joint partners in the Pembroke Cracking Company operation, pleaded guilty at Swansea Crown Court to four charges brought by HSE under Sections 2 and 3 of the Health and Safety at Work Act 1974. The companies were fined a total of £100 000 each, with joint costs of £143 700, for failing to ensure the health and safety of employees, contractors and the public.

CASE 5

The Associated Octel Co. Ltd was prosecuted after a major fire at the company's ethyl chloride (EC) plant at Ellesmere Port, on 1 February 1994. While no one was harmed, the incident caused great concern to local residents and received national publicity because of the explosion risk that, at one stage, was thought to exist. Octel, who pleaded guilty, were fined a total of £150 000 with £142 655 costs for breaches of Sections 2 and 3 of the Health and Safety at Work Act 1974 for failing to provide and maintain plant and systems of work which were safe and without risks to health. As a result, the company put at risk the health and safety of employees and others, particularly the firefighters involved.

Activity 38

Use the cases you have just read to answer the following questions:

1 If an accident is caused by a contractor, is the company that brought in the contractor liable to any penalty?
2 What other costs, apart from a fine, might an organization have to pay if they are successfully prosecuted?
3 Is it necessary for someone to be injured for a company to be prosecuted?

See Feedback section for answer to this activity.

Health and safety policy

The HASAWA states that all organizations with five or more employees must have a health and safety policy statement. This statement should express the organization's aims in relation to the health and safety of employees. It is important that this policy is drawn up in consultation with the people who work for the organization. It cannot succeed without their support and should, as far as possible, reflect their concerns.

A typical health and safety policy contains information on the following topics:

* a general statement expressing a commitment to health and safety
* the name of a senior officer who is responsible for seeing that the policy is implemented and kept under review
* an explanation of who is responsible for safety at various levels of the organization
* a description of how ordinary employees are to be involved in health and safety matters, for example, by taking part in discussions and by sitting on a safety committee
* the procedure for reporting accidents
* fire precautions, fire drill and evacuation procedures
* first aid, including the name and location of the individual responsible for first aid and the location of the first aid box
* safety training
* the inspection of lifts and other equipment
* maintenance of plant and potentially harmful substances
* other hazards
* supervision of employees, especially young and/or inexperienced workers, to ensure their safety
* procedures for risk assessment.

Investigate 32

Obtain a copy of the health and safety policy statement of the organization you work for, or the college at which you are studying.

Does it cover all the points listed above? Does it cover anything else?

Some health and safety policies make quite difficult reading. These documents are sometimes written to reassure the authorities that the organization is taking health and safety seriously. A policy may not be the best way to inform the workforce about health and safety. Posters, leaflets and videos are often more effective. An organization can also show its concern by providing training courses on specific health and safety issues and, more generally, by the time and resources it is willing to devote to this area.

Activity 39

How seriously do you think your organization **really** takes health and safety? Is there anything else you think they ought to be doing?

The majority of organizations make an effort to follow the letter of health and safety legislation, but not all of them follow the spirit!

Safety audit and risk assessment

Safety audits and risk assessments are both forms of safety inspection. As a team leader, it is likely that you will be involved in both. In an audit, the focus is on checking that existing rules are being followed.

A risk assessment takes a wider view. It looks beyond current safety procedures and considers whether there are additional hazards in the workplace and, if so, what action should be taken. A risk assessment should be undertaken when an organization first prepares its safety policy and at regular intervals after that.

HEALTH AND SAFETY

> **How to conduct a risk assessment**
>
> STEP 1
> Look for the hazards
>
> STEP 2
> Decide who might be harmed, and how
>
> STEP 3
> Evaluate the risks arising from the hazards and decide
> whether existing precautions are adequate – or whether
> more should be done
>
> STEP 4
> Record your findings
>
> STEP 5
> Review your assessment from time to time and revise it if
> necessary

Here are some dangers you should look out for in the
workplace:

* Are there any inflammable materials stored near sources of
  heat?
* Are there any hazardous chemicals (including cleaning
  materials) on the premises? Are they stored correctly?
* Can you see any bare electrical wires visible?
* Are there any trailing wires?
* Are extractor fans removing dust?
* Are working areas excessively hot or cold?
* Are working areas too noisy?
* Are the toilets clean?
* Are floors, passages, stairs, etc. clear from obstructions?
* in areas that are open to the public, are there any hazards
  for children?
* If food is prepared on the premises, are the conditions
  hygienic?
* Is food stored at the correct temperature?
* What kind of waste is produced? How is it stored? Does it
  present any potential dangers?

Not all the points in this list will be relevant to your
workplace. There may also be some specific dangers, related
to the type of work that is done there, that need to be
considered.

Activity 40

Draw up a checklist of points to look out for in your own workplace.

In any workplace, there are usually some individuals who organize their workspace to suit themselves. These people can be very defensive about their own territory. In some cases, they may arrange furniture and equipment in ways that are potentially dangerous. When challenged, they may say that they know what they are doing and that *they* have never had an accident. However, very few areas within a workplace are actually private. When you do a safety audit, you need to consider what might happen if other members of staff, including the people who clean the building, or any visitors, came into areas like these. The organization would have to take responsibility for any accidents that happened and has a duty to ensure that potential hazards are minimized.

Checking work practices

You cannot perform an effective safety inspection of an empty building. The way that furniture and equipment is positioned is important, but it will not tell the whole story. It is also essential to see how people actually work. Are certain areas too crowded? Do people carry things that are too heavy for them? Are VDU operators sitting comfortably at their desks? Do people use tools in a dangerous way, or leave them around where unauthorized staff could get hold of them? Do staff, such as messengers, who move around the building understand the dangers in all the areas they enter?

In order to discover risks like these, you need to see a workplace functioning normally. However, a safety inspection is not a normal situation. If staff know that an audit or risk assessment is underway they will naturally take more care with what they do. As a team leader, you should be looking out for potential risks on a daily basis. If you see something that concerns you, it may be important to deal with it immediately.

Here are two quick checks that you can perform:

Using a computer

When you sit at your computer screen, check that:

- your arms are approximately horizontal
- your eyes are at the same height as the top of the VDU
- you have enough space under your desk to move your legs freely.

Lifting

When you lift a heavy object, follow these steps:

- make sure that you are not trying to lift something that is too heavy for you. If it is, use a trolley or get help
- stand close to the object you are lifting
- squat down and take hold of the object
- lift with your legs, not your back
- hold the object close to your body as you are carrying it
- keep your body straight. If you twist round you may damage your back.

When you watch your team working, you may see activities that you believe are potentially dangerous, but be unsure what advice you should give. Your safety representative or safety committee may be able to help in this situation. If they do not have any useful information, it is very likely that the HSE or the appropriate professional or trade organization has some guidance that you can use. If the activity you are worried about concerns a piece of equipment or a commercial product of any kind, the manufacturers should be able to advise you.

Dealing with emergencies

You need to be prepared for emergencies. If you think through in advance the steps that you would take, you will be much less likely to panic when you have to act quickly. For some types of emergency, you will need training that is outside the scope of this book. For example, first aid should only be attempted by someone who has received training from an authorized provider, such as St John Ambulance or the Red Cross.

Dealing with accidents

Within every organization, there should be an appointed person who has some knowledge of first aid.

Investigate 33

Who is responsible for first aid in your workplace? What training has he or she received? How would you contact him or her in an emergency?

The names and extension numbers of staff responsible for first aid should be displayed near your phone. You do not want to have to search for this information in an emergency.

The aims of first aid are simple. They are to:

• preserve life – including your own life, the lives of your colleagues and the life of the casualty
• limit the effects of the condition on the casualty
• if possible, promote the casualty's recovery.

If you attend a first aid course, you will probably have an opportunity to discuss your worries about dealing with accidents in the workplace. Most people are concerned about encountering a situation that they cannot deal with. It is important to remember that first aiders are not expected to work miracles. They should not risk their own safety or that of other people. They are simply trained to take the most constructive action they can until professional help arrives.

First aid involves taking the following steps:

1 assess the situation
2 make the area safe
3 assess all casualties; give emergency aid
4 get help
5 deal with the aftermath.

As you can see, giving emergency aid to casualties is only one part of the process. It is also important for someone with a cool head to take control of the situation and make sure that things are done in the correct order.

If you have the opportunity, it is worth seriously considering taking a first aid course yourself. You will find that it gives you extra confidence about your ability to cope with emergencies - both in the workplace and in your life outside work.

Investigate 34

What organizations run first aid courses in your area? Would your own organization sponsor you to attend a course?

Dealing with fire

All organizations must prepare detailed plans for dealing with fire in the workplace. These plans may be included in the health and safety policy.

The procedure below describes what staff should do if a fire is discovered in a particular college. The procedures in the building where you work will not be exactly the same as these, but they should cover the same general issues.

Raising the Alarm

The alarm should be raised as soon as a fire is discovered, no matter how small. Even if a fire is only suspected, it is essential that all occupants of the building are warned at the earliest opportunity, so that they can make their escape before the fire has time to develop. The following procedure is to be followed.

If a member or staff or a student discovers or suspects an outbreak of fire, he or she should immediately raise the alarm by breaking the glass on a fire alarm point.

The individual who raises the alarm should then immediately contact the switchboard by dialling 0 and then proceed to the assembly point and report details of the incident to the Fire Officer.

The fire alarm consists of the continuous ringing of the fire bells.

Calling the Fire Brigade

The College alarm system is linked automatically to a listening station which is monitored 24 hours a day. The local fire brigade will be summoned immediately the alarm sounds. There is no need to dial 999.

Evacuation of the Buildings

When the fire alarm sounds, everyone should leave the buildings at a brisk walking pace and proceed to the assembly point, which is on the sports field behind the College. It is important not to congregate on, or obstruct, the drive in front of the College because this will be needed as an access route by the fire engines.

Students or members of staff with disabilities should report to the General Office, where they will be assisted from the building, if necessary.

People should leave the building by the doors next to the General Office OR the doors next to the Learning Resources Centre, whichever exit is closer.

The first people to leave by the outside doors should fasten the doors open, in order to expedite the evacuation of the building.

Groups of students should walk together out of the building and not attempt to overtake other groups.

Each lecturer should ensure that all windows and doors are closed and lights are switched off when leaving the classrooms. Students working in unsupervised rooms should be advised that the last person to leave a room should close the door as he or she leaves.

In rooms fitted with gas guard systems, lecturers should use the emergency cut off button as they leave.

No lifts are to be used during the evacuation of the building.

Tackling the Fire

All members of staff should be familiar with the location of the various types of extinguisher and know which type of fire they are intended for. Anyone in the vicinity of the outbreak of fire who is capable of using an extinguisher should tackle the fire, providing s/he does not expose her/himself to any undue risk or danger.

You should **not** continue to fight a fire if:

- it is dangerous to do so
- there is a possibility that your escape route may be cut off by the fire itself or by smoke
- the fire continues to grow, despite your efforts
- there are gas cylinders in the area that may be ignited by the fire.

The first priority is the safe evacuation of all students. It is essential that this is instigated **before** any staff are released to attempt to fight the fire.

Investigate 35

Obtain a copy of the fire procedures that operate in the building where you work or study. Compare it with the example given here and answer these questions:

- What should the person who discovers the fire do first?
- How should the fire brigade be summoned?
- What route should people use to get out of the building?
- Where should people congregate?
- What arrangements are there to check that everyone has got out of the building?
- What arrangements are made for people with disabilities?
- What advice is given to staff about fighting a fire themselves?
- Is there anything in the building (such as inflammable gases or chemicals) that could provide an extra hazard in a fire?

You should also be aware of the various types of fire extinguisher that are available in the building, and the kind of situation in which they should be used.

Types of fire extinguisher

Water
Use for: most solid fires, except those involving live electrical equipment or flammable liquids. Do not use on chip pan fires.

Foam

Use for: most fires involving flammable liquids. Foam is not suitable for all liquids. It is essential to check the instructions. Do not use for chip pan fires.

Dry powder

Use for: fires involving flammable liquids or electrical apparatus. However, dry powder does not penetrate the spaces in equipment easily and it is possible that the fire may flare up again. Do not use for chip pan fires.

Carbon dioxide

Use for: fires involving flammable liquids or electrical apparatus. Carbon dioxide should not be used in confined spaces where there is a danger that the fumes may be inhaled. Do not use for chip pan fires.

Halon

Use for: fires involving flammable liquids or electrical apparatus. May also be used on small surface-burning fires involving solids. Do not use for chip pan fires.

Fire blanket

Use for: fires involving solids and fires involving flammable liquids. Effective for small fires in clothing and chip pan fires, provided that the blanket completely covers the fire.

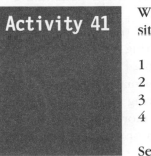

Activity 41

What type of fire extinguisher could be used in these situations?

1 a pile of burning newspapers
2 smoke arising from a computer monitor
3 someone's clothing is alight
4 a chip pan is on fire.

See Feedback section for answer to this activity.

Investigate 36

Examine all the fire extinguishers in the area where you work. What types of fire should they be used on?

HEALTH AND SAFETY

Investigating and reporting accidents

All accidents must be recorded in an accident book. Some injuries must be reported to the authorities on an official form. The Reporting of Injuries, Diseases and Dangerous Occurrences Regulations (RIDDOR) 1995 list the events that must be reported:

- death or major injury to an employee, self-employed person or member of the public
- over-three-day injuries to employees and self-employed people – these are injuries that result in someone being away from work, or unable to do their normal job, for more than three days, including weekends and days when they would not normally be at work
- certain diseases among employees
- dangerous occurrences – such as explosions or spillages of chemicals that could have resulted in a reportable injury, but did not.

Reportable major injuries

These are the major injuries that must be reported:

- fracture other than to fingers, thumbs or toes
- amputation
- dislocation of the shoulder, hip, knee or spine
- loss of sight (temporary or permanent)
- chemical or hot metal burn to the eye or any penetrating injury to the eye
- injury resulting from an electric shock or electrical burn leading to unconsciousness or requiring resuscitation or admittance to hospital for more than 24 hours
- any other injury: leading to hypothermia, heat-induced illness or unconsciousness, or requiring resuscitation, or requiring admittance to hospital for more than 24 hours
- unconsciousness caused by asphyxia or exposure to a harmful substance or biological agent
- acute illness requiring medical treatment, or loss of consciousness arising from absorption of any substance by inhalation, ingestion or through the skin
- acute illness requiring medical treatment where there is reason to believe that this resulted from exposure to a biological agent or its toxins or infected material.

Reportable dangerous occurrences

The following list summarizes some of the dangerous occurrences that must be reported. It is important to remember that these incidents must be reported even if nobody is actually injured:

- the collapse, overturning or failure of load-bearing parts of lifts and lifting equipment
- explosion, collapse or bursting of any closed vessel or associated pipework
- plant or equipment coming into contact with overhead power lines
- an electrical short circuit or overload causing a fire or an explosion
- accidental release of a biological agent likely to cause severe human illness
- the failure of radiography or irradiation equipment to de-energize or return to its safe position after the intended exposure period
- the collapse or partial collapse of a scaffold that is over five metres high or that is erected near water where there could be a risk of drowning after a fall
- a dangerous substance being conveyed by road is involved in a fire or released
- the unintended collapse of: any building or structure under construction, alteration or demolition where over 5 tonnes of material falls
- explosion or fire causing suspension of normal work for over 24 hours
- the accidental release of any substance which may damage health.

Investigate 37

Study the list of reportable dangerous occurrences. Which of them could happen in the place where you work? Are you aware of any of these incidents happening in the past?

Reportable diseases

The list of reportable diseases includes:

- certain poisonings
- some skin diseases
- lung diseases including: occupational asthma, farmer's lung, pneumoconiosis and asbestosis

- infections such as: leptospirosis, hepatitis, tuberculosis, legionellosis and tetanus
- some other conditions such as: occupational cancer, certain musculoskeletal disorders, decompression illness and hand-arm vibration syndrome.

Information about diseases may come from the doctor of the person concerned, or from the person him or herself. If you are not sure whether a disease is reportable, you should telephone the enforcing authority and check.

There are two reasons why these diseases must be reported. Some of these conditions are infectious and could be spread to other people working for the organization, or to the public. Other conditions may indicate that something is happening in the workplace that could affect the health of other people in the future and must therefore be investigated.

Activity 42

Should the following diseases be reported because

(a) they could be transmitted by the person concerned to other people in the workplace, or

(b) they are a sign that the working conditions may be unsafe?

1 asbestosis
2 hepatitis
3 poisoning.

See Feedback section for answer to this activity.

Reporting an incident

The official RIDDOR form asks for details of what happened, including:

- the name of any substance involved
- the name and type of any machine involved
- the events that led up to the incident
- the part played by anyone involved, including the person who was hurt
- action taken to avoid a recurrence of the accident.

The timing of the report is important. If there is a death or a case of major injury, it should be reported by telephoning the enforcing authority without delay. (In most cases, the enforcing authority is the local authority.) Within ten days you should follow up this conversation by sending in a completed accident report form (F2508). Dangerous occurrences should be treated in the same way as deaths and major injuries. You should telephone immediately and then send in an accident report form within ten days. An over-three-day injury does not require a telephone call, but it should also be reported on an accident report form within ten days. Diseases should be reported on a different form (F2508A).

Summary

The two most important organizations concerned with health and safety are the Health and Safety Commission and the Health and Safety Executive. You may also be able to obtain specialist advice from your trade association or the professional body responsible for your industry. The Health and Safety at Work Act 1974 lists the responsibilities of employers and employees. Penalties under health and safety legislation can include fines and even imprisonment. Organizations who break the rules can also suffer financially if they have to pay compensation or legal costs, or through the commercial effects of bad publicity.

All organizations with more than five employees must have a health and safety policy. Organizations should perform regular safety audits and risk assessments. As a team leader, you should be constantly aware of potential risks in your area of responsibility. You should know who to contact within the organization if there is an accident. Better still, you should take first aid training yourself. You must also be familiar with the procedures that should be followed in case of fire. Any accident that results in death or serious injury, also three-day-injuries, certain diseases and certain dangerous occurrences, should be reported to the authorities.

Review and discussion questions

1 What is the role of the HSE?
2 Under the HASAWA 1974, what are the general responsibilities of employers?
3 What is the difference between a safety audit and a risk assessment?
4 What are the basic aims of first aid?
5 What is a three-day-injury and how should it be reported?

HEALTH AND SAFETY

Case study

Meryl is a team leader in an office block. She has no particular responsibilities for health and safety. She describes an incident that happened to her recently:

The caretaker had a little room in the basement. I had worked in the building for over a year before I knew the room was there. However, one evening I was working late and had to go down and ask him for the key to the archive cupboard. When he opened his door, I saw that on one side of the room there were piles of old newspapers. There was an old-fashioned two-bar electric fire right next to them. If the papers had slipped onto the fire, the whole place could have gone up. What is more, the caretaker was smoking and I could see cigarette burns on the upholstery of his armchair. There was a cat sleeping in front of the fire and there were empty tins of catfood stacked up by the door. There was a television balanced on a pile of newspapers and the wire trailed over to the socket at ankle height. A safety chain had been fitted to the inside of the door, so that it could only be opened from the inside when the caretaker was in there. I also saw an opened carton of cleaning materials on the floor, with a dark stain on the carpet next to them.

The caretaker could see that I was a bit taken aback and I felt that I had to make some comment. All I said was, 'Are you sure that television's safe up there?' He replied, 'Nobody comes in this room but me, so I don't want anyone telling me about health and safety. I've kept my things how I want them for 30 years and I'm not about to start changing them now.'

What would you do in Meryl's situation?

Work-based assignment

Assess the risks to health and safety for your team. What extra information or guidance do members of your team need? Obtain copies of any leaflets, posters, checklists or other material that will be of use.

Action plan

This action plan can be used to carry out a risk assessment with your team.

1 Call a meeting and talk to your team about potential risks and the responsibilities of employers and employees under the HASAWA.
2 Ask everyone to be aware of potential risks over the next week.
3 Have another meeting and establish areas of concern.
4 Where it is possible, revise work procedures to avoid these risks to health.
5 Where necessary, report your team's concerns to your own manager in writing and ask for comments.

6 The environment

Learning objectives

On completion of this chapter you will be able to:

- describe the role of the Environment Agency
- outline significant measures in the Environmental Protection Act
- list other environmental legislation
- describe methods of reducing pollution
- describe methods of conserving natural resources
- describe methods of conserving energy.

NVQ links

This chapter covers much of the underpinning knowledge required for the vocational qualification in management at level 3 for the optional units:

Unit E5 Identify improvements to energy efficiency

which consists of two elements

E5.1   Identify opportunities to improve energy efficiency
E5.2   Recommend improvements to energy efficiency

Unit E8 Provide advice and support for improving energy efficiency

which consists of three elements

E8.1   Encourage involvement in energy efficiency activities
E8.2   Provide advice on the competencies needed to use energy efficiently
E8.3   Provide advice on the training needed to use energy efficiently

Introduction

As an individual, you may or may not have strong feelings about the environment. You may be one of those people who use bottle banks, buy items made from recycled paper and avoid using aerosols. Or these things may not be particularly important to you.

Increasingly, care for the environment is becoming more than a personal decision. The Government, and many major national organizations, are taking steps to encourage everyone, including industry and business, to take green issues seriously. This is being done partly through legislation, partly through financial and other incentives and partly through information and education. For example, many organizations now ask potential suppliers for evidence that their materials and work practices are 'environmentally friendly'. If your organization has not yet addressed these issues, it may be at a commercial disadvantage.

Most forms of energy generation cause pollution of some kind. The conservation of energy is therefore something that environmentalists want to promote. Energy savings can also result in significant economies for the organizations that make them.

If you are already interested in environmental issues, this chapter may give you some more ideas for measures that you can take in the workplace. The actions you take here are likely to influence a much wider range of people than the things you do to conserve energy and resources at home. If you are not committed to caring for the environment, this chapter may perhaps convince you that it is time that you took these issues more seriously.

Environmental legislation

The UK Government believes that environmental improvements should be achieved by a combination of regulation, economic instruments and voluntary action. The regulation arm of this approach is the responsibility of the Environment Agency and local authorities.

The Environment Agency

The Environment Agency for England and Wales describes itself as 'one of the most powerful environmental regulators in the world'. This organization is the result of a merger between the National Rivers Authority, Her Majesty's Inspectorate of Pollution, the Waste Regulation Authorities and some smaller units from the Department of the Environment. By bringing together the expertise and experience of these different organizations, the Environment Agency hopes to provide an integrated approach to environmental matters. The responsibilities of the Environment Agency include:

- regulating over 2000 industrial processes that have the potential to cause pollution
- advising national and local government on air quality management
- regulating the disposal of radioactive waste
- regulating the treatment and disposal of controlled waste
- preserving and improving the quality of rivers
- regulating the management and improvement of contaminated land.

The Environment Agency authorizes industrial processes under the integrated pollution control system (IPC) and can suspend operations and prosecute businesses.

Local authorities

Businesses that want to develop land or change its use must apply for permission to the local authority. The town and country planning legislation includes detailed guidance on the environmental requirements for various types of development. Certain types of activity, such as oil refineries, power stations and chemical installations, are subject to a process entitled Environmental Assessment. Potential developers must publish information about the likely environmental impact of their proposals.

Legislation

The most important piece of legislation is the Environmental Protection Act 1990. Among other measures, this makes waste producers responsible for the safe management and disposal of waste until it is taken care of by an appropriate waste management organization. A duty of care is imposed on all those involved in the production and disposal of waste. Fines are unlimited and offenders can be imprisoned for up to two years.

In the past, organizations that produced waste were not responsible for what happened to it once it had been removed from their premises. This meant that dangerous and toxic substances could be dumped, by unscrupulous operators, in places where they could do great environmental damage. Now businesses are responsible for ensuring that their waste is dealt with by an organization that is authorized to dispose of it. It is hoped that this will result in businesses taking the question of waste much more seriously.

The Environmental Protection Act also introduces a concept known as Integrated Pollution Control (IPC). Businesses that carry out potentially damaging industrial processes must select a manufacturing process and a method of disposal of waste products that ensure the least effects on the environment as a whole.

Another important concept in the Act is the requirement for organizations to use the 'best available techniques not entailing excessive costs' (BATNEEC). The details of these techniques are not defined. This means that new demands can be made on industry as improved techniques become available.

The Environmental Protection Act makes a distinction between different types of business. Part A business are those carrying out potentially damaging industrial processes, such as those involving asbestos, cement manufacture, oil or metal refining and chemical processes.

Part B businesses are those carrying out less dangerous operations, but on a scale large enough to cause some risk to the environment. Part B processes do not have to face such rigorous controls. However, they are subject to controls on their emissions to the atmosphere. There are also other businesses that are classified as neither Part A or Part B.

Businesses also need to be aware of the following legislation:

- Environment Act 1995
- Town and Country Planning Act 1990
- Town and Country Planning (Assessment of Environmental Effects) Regulations 1988
- Planning (Hazardous Substances) Act 1990
- Control of Pollution (Special Regulations) 1980
- Water Resources Act 1991
- Water Industry Act 1991
- Health and Safety at Work Act 1974.

All of these pieces of legislation may have implications for your organization.

THE ENVIRONMENT

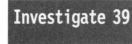

Investigate 38 Describe the main activities of the organization that you work for. In what ways do you think these activities present dangers to the environment? What pieces of legislation apply to your organization?

Sources of pollution

When we think about pollution, we normally think of major disasters such as oil spillages, the emission of poison gases into the atmosphere or the leaching of dangerous chemicals into the soil. If the organization you work for is engaged in industrial processes, it may present large-scale hazards of this kind to the environment. However, if you do work for an organization like this, senior management will, almost certainly, already have addressed these potential problems. In this section, we will concentrate on the smaller-scale sources of pollution that are relevant to all organizations. It is in these areas that you, as a team leader, are likely to have more impact in making improvements.

Hazardous materials

If your organization uses hazardous chemicals of any kind, it should arrange proper storage facilities. When these chemicals are safely locked up in a cupboard or storeroom, they present little danger. However, it is also important to consider what could happen if the storage facilities are damaged in any way. For example, what would happen if the building was flooded? What would happen if the building caught fire?

Hazardous materials can also present a danger when they are arriving at or leaving the premises. It is important that people involved in loading or unloading and transporting these materials know what they are dealing with, and what they should do in case of an accident.

While an organization may have made careful plans to deal with accidents, these plans may have been formulated some time ago. It is possible that the staff who are currently employed have not been trained in what to do.

Investigate 39 Find out what hazardous materials are kept on the premises where you work. What plans have been made to deal with accidents? Who knows the details of these plans?

ACTIVITIES MANAGEMENT

CFC gases

Chlorofluorocarbon gases, commonly known as CFCs, are used in refrigerator coolants, aerosols, air conditioning units, many foams and polystyrene packing. CFCs are thought to have a significant role in climate change. The contribution of a molecule of CFC towards the greenhouse effect is *ten thousand* times greater than the contribution of a molecule of carbon dioxide.

CFCs also destroy the ozone layer. The ozone layer acts as a sort of shield, protecting the earth from ultraviolet radiation from the sun. If the ozone layer is damaged, plants and plankton in the sea can receive too much ultraviolet radiation and die. The ozone layer is crucial to the survival of life on earth.

Investigate 40

Look around the office in which you work. How many of the materials you use contain CFCs? How many of them are essential to your work?

Traffic pollution

Your organization probably uses vehicles of some kind. Even if it does not, you and your colleagues are likely to use cars to get to work. This is an area where an organization can make a significant impact on pollution. Here are some suggestions:

- organize a car-sharing pool, so that people do not travel to work in their cars alone
- encourage people to use public transport whenever possible when they travel on behalf of the organization
- supplement public transport with a company minibus
- make sure that any vehicles purchased for the organization are as environmentally friendly as possible
- provide bicycle racks and showers to encourage those who can to cycle to and from work
- strongly discourage people from using messenger services to deliver one or two packages at a time
- if appropriate, allow some members of staff to work at home on occasions.

THE ENVIRONMENT

> **Investigate 41**   Conduct a survey on your colleagues. How many of them drive to work? What would persuade them to use an alternative form of transport?

Conserving natural resources

The greenhouse effect is caused by an increase in the level of carbon dioxide in the atmosphere. Carbon dioxide retains heat. As levels rise, the earth's atmosphere heats up. As you are probably aware, it is feared that this rise in temperature will melt the polar ice caps, causing sea levels to rise, changing the pattern of currents in the oceans and bringing about other climate changes.

Carbon dioxide is produced by the burning of fossil fuels, such as petrol, coal, gas or oil. In past centuries, the forests of the world kept the system in balance by turning back carbon dioxide into oxygen and vegetation. However, the forests of the world are disappearing. An area about the size of England, Wales and Northern Ireland is cut down every year. There are several ways in which businesses can act to slow down this process:

- refuse to buy (or sell) any furniture or other items that are made from non-sustainable hardwoods
- avoid battery-powered equipment or anything that requires materials that are obtained by mining areas that are currently covered in forest
- avoid doing business with foreign countries who are involved in deforestation
- use recycled paper wherever possible
- avoid any unnecessary use of fossil fuels.

You may be able to influence the use of paper in your office. Here is an account of some measures that were taken by one office manager:

First of all, I made sure that we used chlorine-free recycled paper for all our company correspondence. I also encouraged everyone to use e-mail whenever they could, instead of putting things in a written memo. There were also several long documents that were regularly sent to a large number of people within the company. This was completely unnecessary, as people did not need their own copies of this material. I encouraged the managers concerned to put these documents on the Intranet, so that anybody who needed to consult them could have instant access. I also looked at the fax machines and, when it was time to replace them, I selected models that would print on both sides of the paper. And then I started a policy of not including a cover sheet with faxes. A tremendous amount of paper could be saved if people just put a header at the top of their first page of text.

I also looked at the paper that we generated in the office. We had quite a few booklets and leaflets printed over the year. I spoke to the company that did this for us and made sure that they used a water miscible varnish that made the paper easier to recycle. On the booklets, we used a water-based adhesive for the same reasons.

Activity 43	Now make a list of the things you could do in the office where you work to reduce the amount of paper that is used.

Almost anything that is manufactured causes a depletion of the earth's natural resources. It is good practice for organizations to recycle any equipment, components, or materials that they can. Unfortunately, many businesses have a culture in which people's status is measured by the 'newness' of the furniture and equipment that they use.

If you take measures to conserve natural resources, you should tell your customers and suppliers what you are doing. This may get you extra business. It will also help spread the message that conservation is something that is now being taken seriously by an increasing number of organizations.

Conserving energy

Electricity is the main source of power in most businesses today. Much of this electricity is produced by burning fossil fuels and therefore makes a significant contribution to the greenhouse effect. As far as the management of your organization is concerned, saving energy is likely to be one of the most popular conservation measures because it also saves money.

If you are looking at energy use in your organization, you need to consider:

- the way that people use energy
- the equipment that is provided
- the premises themselves.

Use of energy

Many people think that, because they are not paying for energy themselves, it does not matter how much they use. You may have experienced incidents like these:

> *I came into work very early one winter morning to finish off an important report. I was amazed to see that every light in the building was switched on. The cleaners were working in the offices and had turned on all the lights at once. They were only working on a floor at a time, so this represented a tremendous waste of electricity. I asked what time they started. It was 5 a.m. So the whole block had been lit for an extra four hours before the day-time staff got into work! And I suspect that this happened every day.*

> *I walked into the computer suite. It was a large room, with about twenty machines. Every single one of them was turned on, with a screensaver slowly turning on the screen. The printer was also switched on. There was only one person working in the room. A manager was sitting at the far end – and he was actually writing some notes on a pad of paper.*

> *The hot water tap in the washroom was dripping. Something had gone wrong with the washer. I felt the water that was coming out – it was warm. So the boiler was being used to heat water that was going straight down the drain.*

People may need reminding from time to time of the cost of the energy that they are using. One way to do this is to put stickers on light switches and equipment. Another way, which could be more effective, is for departmental managers to know more about the 'overheads' that they are responsible for. If a method can be found to reflect energy savings in the budgets that are available to different parts of an organization, the subject may seem more relevant and important.

Equipment

Office equipment uses a great deal of energy. Much of it is not in use for a vast proportion of the time that it is switched on. A typical fax machine is used for one hour a day. A printer usually stands idle for 95 per cent of the time. And yet these machines are normally left switched on all the time. It is possible to buy faxes, printers, computers, monitors and copiers that 'go to sleep' when they are not being used, making great savings of energy. Here are two examples:

- a monitor that turns itself off can save between 60 per cent and 80 per cent of the power it uses
- a computer with a similar facility can use over 50 per cent less energy.

Investigate 42

Find out how much your organization pays for electricity. Also find out how much power the electronic equipment in your office uses. Work out how much money could be saved by using equipment that reverted to a low-power state when it was not in use.

When new electronic equipment is being purchased, make sure that the specification includes a requirement that the equipment uses as little energy as possible. If you work in a small office, you should also consider whether equipment that performs several functions, such as a printer that doubles as a fax machine and a scanner, could be used to save energy.

Premises

You probably will not be able to change the premises in which your organization works, but you may have some influence on the way they are maintained. Leaky taps, draughty windows and doors that are left open can all increase the energy bill. Also consider the temperature in the workplace. Is it so hot that people are forced to open the windows? If the workplace is heated by radiators, is it possible to regulate the temperature of individual radiators? Many workplaces are far too hot for comfort.

THE ENVIRONMENT

Summary

The Environment Agency is responsible for regulating industrial processes and the disposal of waste. It has also taken on the powers of other agencies, such as the National Rivers Authority and Her Majesty's Inspectorate of Pollution. The most important piece of environmental legislation in recent years is the Environmental Protection Act 1990. This introduced two important concepts: integrated pollution control and 'best available techniques not entailing excessive costs'.

The greenhouse effect is central to the concerns of environmentalists. This is believed to be caused by the increase in carbon dioxide in the atmosphere and is exacerbated by gases such as CFCs that destroy the ozone layer. Businesses can help to slow down this effect by conserving natural resources and conserving energy. If you take action in this area, you will probably also save your organization money. What is more, your actions may have an effect on your customers and your suppliers and you will help raise the profile of green issues generally.

Review and discussion questions

1 Why is the principle of 'best available techniques not entailing excessive costs' important?
2 Why are CFCs so destructive?
3 Suggest three ways in which you could reduce the traffic pollution caused by the people who work for your organization.
4 What kind of paper is best for recycling?
5 What energy-saving features should you specify when a new piece of electronic equipment is purchased?

Case study

Saul is the manager of a medium-sized office building on the outskirts of a town. The company produces catalogues and mailshots for a variety of different organizations. Fifty people are employed on the premises, most of whom drive to work. The company has not yet invested very much money in IT. There are a few stand-alone PCs in the building, but most staff use word-processors. The building is heated by radiators, powered by an oil-fired boiler in the basement. The whole building is quite old and in need of refurbishment.

Saul has just seen a television programme about global warming and, for the first time in his life, realizes that this is a problem that will soon concern him. He would like to do something about it, but does not know what impact one person can have.

What would you say to Saul?

Work-based assignment

Write a memo to your manager suggesting six practical and inexpensive ways in which your organization could improve the effect that it has on the environment.

Action plan

This action plan can be used to increase your team's awareness of how their work activities affect the environment.

1 Ask people to log the amount of paper they use and then to reduce this amount by 25 per cent.
2 Ask for suggestions of methods of reducing energy consumption in the workplace.
3 Start collecting goods for recycling (such as aluminium cans) in the workplace.
4 Draw up a 'green list' of questions for new suppliers of materials and equipment.

Feedback

Activity 1

There are five suppliers: the market garden, the wholesaler, the supermarket group, the individual supermarket and the customer.

Activity 3

A and B account for about 80 per cent of the reasons why customers did not renew their service contracts. The company needs to focus on why the representatives do not turn up on time. This may involve improving the appointment system. They should also improve the quality of customer information, so that people understand the importance of having their central heating system serviced regularly.

Activity 6

The most risky strategy is unrelated diversification, because an organization is dealing with untried products in an unfamiliar market. Because the organization cannot rely on past experience, it is more likely to make mistakes. By the same logic, market consolidation and penetration are considered to be the least risky strategies.

Activity 12

1 If the invoice has not been signed.
2 If there is no matching purchase order or the amounts and job descriptions do not agree.
3 No, because invoices are coded, photocopied and then the copy is filed.

Activity 14   All the tasks except **check copy** lie on the critical path.

Activity 17
1 is a problem at the input stage.
2 is a problem that is not discovered until the output stage.
3 is a problem that comes to light during the process itself.

Activity 18   You might need to check:

1 the special envelopes: have they arrived? Do they match the specifications you gave the stationer? Are there enough? Does the invoice correspond to the price you were quoted?
2 the set of addresses from the database: are there any duplications? Are the addresses complete? Is the task complete?
3 1000 copies of the letter: have they arrived? How good are the copies?
4 the addressed envelopes: are the addresses correctly positioned on the envelopes? Are there any blanks? Is the task complete?
5 the filled envelopes: are the letters neatly folded? Are there any empty envelopes? Is the task complete?
6 the franked envelopes: have any envelopes been missed? Is the task complete?
7 certificate of postage: is it for the correct number of items? Were the envelopes posted on the expected day?

Activity 19   Your answers will reflect the situation in which you work, but you would probably be happy to let experienced members of your team monitor routine activities. Situations where you would need to monitor yourself might include new tasks, the work done by new members of staff and any situations where there had recently been problems and situations where the reputation of your team was at stake.

Activity 21
1 You should have added together the variance in volume for each item. The answer is 401.
2 You should have added together the variance in value for each item. The answer is £3026.90.

Activity 22
1 The actual spending is higher than the budgeted spending, so the project is more expensive than expected.

2 If you look at the two lines carefully, you can see that they follow a similar shape. However, the actual line is a little to the right of the budget line. This suggests that money is being spent as predicted, but slightly later than was planned. It looks as though the project is about a month behind schedule.

Activity 23

1 The warehouse problem was probably caused by people who did not understand the process.
2 The rota problem was caused by a process that caused difficulties for people.

Activity 24

Here are some possible solutions:

- allow the team members who did not like the new rota to hand in their notice
- abandon the new rota altogether
- amend the system to fit in with the wishes of staff.

The best solution is probably to be more flexible with the system.

Activity 25

You should have been able to think of several disadvantages:

- you will have to brief everyone and check their work
- people may not do the task in exactly the same way, so you may have problems with consistency
- the people you bring in will not be able to get on with their ordinary work. If you hire them especially, they will cost you extra money
- people take a certain amount of time to learn a new task and may not be as quick as the person who is doing it already
- you may demotivate the person who is working on the task already.

Activity 34

1 continuous process
2 batch production
3 project or jobbing production.

Activity 36

A: 7; B: 2; C: 4; D: 3, 4; E: 5; F: 6, 7; G: 1, 7.

Activity 37

Advantages include:

- convenience, because staff requiring supplies have shorter distances to travel
- goods requiring different storage conditions can be kept separately
- departments can manage their own supplies.

Disadvantages include:

- reduced levels of security
- reduced levels of stock control
- extra cost, if storage facilities are duplicated.

Activity 38

1 If the client company has not briefed the contractor properly, or has been negligent in some other way, they may be penalized even more heavily than the contractor.
2 A company may have costs awarded against it in court. This can be even more expensive than the fine itself. If negligence has been proved, insurance companies may refuse to compensate the company for any loss. You may also have thought of the commercial losses that can arise as a result of the bad publicity following an accident and a court case.
3 No, it is not necessary for anyone to be injured for a company to be prosecuted.

Activity 41

1 Water or a fire blanket
2 Carbon dioxide or halon
3 Fire blanket
4 Fire blanket.

Activity 42

1 (b); 2 (a); 3 (b).

Further reading

Belbin, M. (1981) *Management Teams: Why they Succeed or Fail*, Butterworth-Heinemann

Dixon, R. (1994) *The Management Task*, Butterworth-Heinemann and the Institute of Management Foundation

Essentials of health and safety at work, HSE Books. The HSE produces a wide range of leaflets and information sheets dealing with specific risks or types of work. You can view these on their website (http://www.open.gov.uk/hse/hsehome.htm) or order printed copies from the HSE.

First Aid Manual (7th Edition) (1997) The Authorized Manual of St John Ambulance, St Andrew's Ambulance Association, and the British Red Cross, Dorling Kindersley

Fowler, E. and Graves, P. (1995) *Managing an Effective Operation*, Butterworth-Heinemann and the Institute of Management Foundation

Gedye, R. (1979) *Works Management and Productivity*, William Heinemann Ltd

Lake, C. (1997) *Mastering Project Management*, Thorogood Ltd

Macdonald, J. (1993) *Understanding Total Quality Management in a Week*, Hodder & Stoughton and the Institute of Management Foundation

Munro-Faure, L., Munro-Faure, M. and Bones, E. (1993) *Achieving Quality Standards: A Step-by-step Guide to BS5750/ISO900*, Pitman Publishing and the Institute of Management Foundation

Taylor, B., Hutchinson, C., Pollack, S. and Tapper, R. (1994) *Environmental Management Handbook*, Pitman Publishing and the Institute of Management Foundation

Wheatley, M. (1992) *Understanding Just in Time in a Week*, Hodder & Stoughton and Institute of Management Foundation

Wheatley, M. (1993) *Green Business: Making it Work for your Company*, Pitman Publishing and the Institute of Management Foundation

Index

Accidents, 127-8, 132
Action plans, 35
Ansoff, 33
Automatic monitoring, 65

Batch production, 98
Belbin, 74
Brainstorming, 11
BS5750, 16
Budget, 31

CFC gases, 143
Change control, 80-1
Checklists, 47
Conserving energy, 145
Contingency allowance, 77
Continuous production, 98-9
Control of Substances Hazardous to Health
    Regulations, 114
COSHH, *see* Control of Substances Hazardous to
    Health Regulations
Critical path analysis, 52
Crosby, 10
Customer requirements, 5
Customer/supplier chain, 4
Customers, 3

Deming, 9
Drucker, 40

Emergencies, 126-31
Environment Agency, 139-40
Environment Protection Act, 1990, 140
Environmental legislation, 140-1
Ergonomics, 87

Fire, 128-31
Fire extinguishers, 130-1
Fishbone diagrams, 13
Flow process chart, 84
Flowcharts, 48-50
Forecasting, 38-9

Gantt charts, 46-7, 53-5
Greenhouse effect, 144

Hazardous materials, 142
Health and Safety at Work Act, 114, 117-19, 122
Health and Safety Commission, 113
Health and Safety Executive, 113
Health and safety legislation, 114, 115
Health and safety policy, 122-3
Herzberg, 87
HSC, *see* Health and Safety Commission
HSE, *see* Health and Safety Executive
Hygiene factors, 87

Impact analysis form, 80
Indexed four quarter moving average, 39
Internal customers, 4
Internal suppliers, 4
ISO9000, 16-19

JIT, *see* Just in time
Jobbing shop production, 97
Juran, 10
Just in time, 99-101

Kabans, 100

Last period forecasting, 39
Learning curve, 41

McClelland, 88
Management by objectives, 35
Meetings, 45-9, 66
Method study, 83-6
Methods of organizing production, 97-101
Mission statement, 32
Motion economy, 86-7
Moving average forecasting, 39

Network diagrams, 50-3

Objectives, 40
Operational plans, 34

Pareto analysis, 12
Planning cycle, 30
Planning process, 27–9
Pollution, 142–3
Problem solving, 72–4
Procedures, 20
Processes, 7
Projects, 81, 82
Purchasing systems, 93–4

Quality gurus, 9–11
Quality management, 20
Quality standards, 15
Quality tools, 11–15

Receiving goods, 103–5
Reportable dangerous occurrences, 133
Reportable diseases, 133–4
Reportable major injuries, 132
Reporting of Injuries, Diseases and Dangerous
        Occurrences Regulations, 132–5
Reports, 67
RIDDOR, *see* Reporting of Injuries, Diseases and
        Dangerous Occurrences Regulations
Risk assessment, 123–5

Safety audits, 123
Sale of Goods Act, 103
Schedules, 31, 46
Self-monitoring, 65
Sensitivity analysis, 63
Specifications, 95
Statistical Process Control, 13
STEP factors, 37
Stock control, 101–3
Storage, 108
Strategic plans, 33
Suppliers, 3
SWOT analysis, 38

Time study, 89
Total Quality Management, 9
TQM, *see* Total Quality Management
Traffic pollution, 143

Unfair Contract Terms Act, 104

Variance, 31, 67

Weighted moving average forecasting, 39
Work instructions, 20
Work study techniques, 83–9